Play From Your Heart

Play From Your Heart

A JOURNEY THROUGH LOSS, RESILIENCE, AND THE BEAUTIFUL GAME

SCOTT MARTIN

CORYANNE HICKS

LIBRARY TALES PUBLISHING

Library Tales Publishing

www.LibraryTalesPublishing.com

For technical support, please visit www.LibraryTalesPublishing.com

Library Tales Publishing also publishes its books in a variety of electronic formats. Every content that appears in print is available in electronic books.

9798894410395
9798894410852

Printed in the United States of America

Contents

One

NIKE

As part of his doctoral thesis, a young assistant professor asked each head coach of every sports team at the university I attended as an undergraduate to select one athlete to be tested for overall strength and fitness to determine the "top athlete" for the men's and women's athletic programs. I was chosen to represent the soccer team. We lifted weights, ran sprints and distance, conducted agility and quickness drills, and measured oxygen intake and heart rates. At the end, the coaches chose a winner: me.

How the fuck did I get here?

With thin clouds and a blue sky overhead, I sailed down I-90 toward Chicago with my tortoiseshell Ray-Bans on and John Mellencamp's *Whenever We Wanted* album blaring through the Bose sound system. It was 1993, and even though new cars like mine were starting to offer CD players, I still loved my cassettes.

The sun had warmed the cornfield landscape to a balmy eighty degrees. Like my car, I too was in overdrive, fueled by the

1

taste of success as I headed to the Nike regional soccer camp, where a hundred of the top high-school players from the Midwest awaited. Not even the tolls on Illinois's main highways—or the fact that my teams always wore adidas—could bring me down.

Early on in my life, I learned that it's not what you know but who you know—and the invitation to speak at the camp made me think of Jon (Yon), who had taken me under his wing during my first coaching gig in Europe the summer after graduation.

Back then, Jon was the director of the academy in the Netherlands where my boys' team, composed of players from across the United States, trained in preparation for our upcoming European tournament schedule.

Seven years later, before taking my position as head women's soccer coach at the University of Wisconsin at Eau Claire, our paths crossed again at another training center in Holland. My career seemed to be flying like a jet, and his like a rocket—he'd become the manager (head coach) of the Dutch Olympic Team.

During our final night at the training center outside Amsterdam, as we sat at a local pub, Jon placed his empty pint of beer on the bar.

"Not all Americans are ignorant of the game. You know what you're talking about, Scott."

I replied with a sheepish, "Thank you, Jon," stretching it to allow for consideration of it as a question.

He rested his hand on my shoulder, looked me in the eye, and said, "I know some people in the States who can help your career."

I think he made good on his promise through Nike.

It was shaping up to be one hell of a summer. We had just wrapped up our final set of youth camps at UW–Eau Claire, and I was heading into year two of running the program. Following the Nike camp, I was heading back to Europe with a group of college players that a coaching buddy and I had handpicked from across the country.

Our itinerary would include one week of training outside Amsterdam, followed by competing in the Holland Cup, the

Dana Cup, and the Gothia Cup in Sweden. *If I ran into Jon again, I'd be buying the beer.*

At thirty-five years old, everything felt right on track. I'd chosen to begin my career as a head coach at a Division III university rather than as someone's assistant at a Division I school. I had a vision of what I wanted to build—I didn't want to be asked to fit into someone else's philosophy. From there, I'd work my way up the coaching ladder to head coach at a Division I college.

My ladder was certainly not straight. With only my initial degree in physical education, I had many doors slammed in my face. Even though high school soccer was taking off, phys-ed teachers tended to coach more "traditional" sports like football or basketball. No one wanted to waste a physical education position on a soccer coach.

I was three years removed from college and languishing as a high school substitute teacher while running the school's soccer program. Admittedly, being shut out from teaching full-time eventually helped prepare me for what was to come. But I liked being in the classroom more than in the gymnasium—and almost as much as on the field.

So, I pivoted: in one academic year, I crammed nearly fifty credits into my schedule, in between subbing, playing, and coaching, to earn my license to teach social studies and history. Finally, I had my own classroom, teaching five periods of Global Studies and running both the boys' and girls' soccer programs in West Bend, Wisconsin.

But I still had climbing left to do; this was only my resting spot before heaving myself up further toward coaching at the college level. Our team at UW–Eau Claire had already received national recognition during my first season. Nothing seemed out of reach.

Success that year, for me, required bringing home the national championship—and I was dead set on doing just that. *I tended to simplify Thomas Paine's statement, "Lead, follow, or get out of the way," to simply, "Get out of the way."*

I was in the prime of my life, both physically and mentally. My coaching trip to Europe the year prior had included Jon inviting me to scrimmage against the Dutch Olympic Team, along with a couple of other playing opportunities, so I put myself on the same training regimen I'd followed during college.

Rotating weightlifting with cardio, along with daily stretching and ball work, had me at an even one-eighty with seven percent body fat and a resting heart rate of thirty-six beats per minute. It seemed like I was in the best shape of my life. *I should have had nothing to worry about.*

Soon, I was hanging a right outside The Windy City toward my hotel, with the trumpet from Mellencamp's "Love and Happiness" ringing in the air. I could still hear that horn in my ears when I awoke the next day to drive out to the Nike camp, a bit tired and headachy from the journey and from the volume of the music I'd played along the way.

The Nike complex was a quarter mile off the main road, encircled by a deep wood. Oak trees towered over single-story, rustic buildings stained a medium brown to match the tree bark. Where there weren't trees or buildings, groomed soccer fields lined the road.

As I drove past, I counted six fields in all. Each had four portable goals scattered in various spots around the green. The air smelled of fresh-cut grass and promise.

As my tires crunched over the gravel parking lot, the door of the main building swung open. A man stepped out, sporting head-to-toe royal-and-black Nike attire. He lifted a hand toward his receding hairline to shade his eyes before raising it to wave.

"Scott Martin?" he asked when I stepped out of the car. "I'm Cliff, the program director. Come on in. We're just finishing up breakfast."

I followed him inside, where we were welcomed by a din to rival my stereo. The gymnasium, which doubled as a dining hall, was filled with teenage boys and girls dressed in blue Nike uniforms. They were all entering their junior or senior year of high school and played on select teams from across the country; many also played on regional Olympic Development Program teams.

The crème of the crop, so to speak. The salesman in me recognized this as the opportunity it was.

According to NCAA rules, I couldn't officially recruit at the event, but I made a point of letting the female players know about UW–Eau Claire. My job wasn't just to sell the soccer program; I was asking student-athletes to make a four-year commitment to prepare them for life after their undergraduate degrees.

I followed Cliff around the outskirts of the room, nabbing a slice of toast and some orange juice from the cafeteria-style breakfast buffet. He led me toward the coaches' table near the front window. My triple-black Pontiac glinted in the parking lot outside.

"Everyone, meet Scott Martin," Cliff said. "He's here to speak about balancing studies with soccer and college recruiting at tonight's forum."

I prioritized academics. Back in the soccer office at UW–Eau Claire, I had framed a statement that hung on a wall that read:

Know Your Priorities:
Family
Studies
Soccer
Social Life

I took a seat at the coaches' table. I recognized a few faces from soccer websites and television, plus some members of the U.S. National Team. If the kids here were at the top of their division, these coaches were just as highly ranked.

"Now that we're all here," Cliff said, "let's go over the plan for the day. We'll have the usual station work in the morning, but since it's our last full day, the afternoon will be cut short for a coaches' match. Scott, you're welcome to participate if you'd like."

"Couldn't say no to that," I replied.

"Great. We'll have someone get you cleats." Before I could tell him that I had brought my own (no soccer rat worth his tail travels without his cleats), Cliff added, "And a Nike uniform."

I glanced down at my shirt emblazoned with the adidas logo and suppressed a grin.

My morning was divided between observing and participating in a few small drills. It was great to witness the creativity of the national team players. They became more artist than player when allowed to freelance away from the structure of their coaches' teachings.

Later, as lunch ended and everyone began to filter out of the cafeteria, I noticed that my legs felt particularly fatigued. Getting up from my chair felt like rising from the bench during a halftime break in the third match of a weekend tournament. The muscles on the left side of my chest, which I had pulled while weight training earlier in the week, protested as I used my arms to push myself up from the table. *Surely the injury was minor—hardly worth thinking about.*

"Scott, feel free to jump in," Cliff said, gesturing to where the other coaches were grouping players to begin a tactical training session.

My thighs quivered. "That's all right," I said. "I think I'll just watch this round."

I moved to a bench in the shade of an oak tree and surreptitiously leaned against it. By the time the training session was over, I'd given up hiding my fatigue altogether and slumped tiredly on the bench.

As the kids cleared the balls from the field, one of the other coaches jogged over to where I sat.

"We're gonna start the coaches' match," she said. "You still in?"

I pushed to my feet, smiling through the leg pain. "You bet."

We broke into teams. *Playing on the left will limit my work rate,* I thought. As it turned out, not enough. Barely ten minutes in, I was panting as if I'd been running for hours. I slid a pass to a teammate for a goal, then doubled over to rest my hands on my knees on the ground.

I was constantly telling my players never to do this because it sent a message to your opponent that you were fatigued. *But something was wrong.*

"Scott, you all right, man?" one of the other coaches asked.

I nodded and tried to give a thumbs-up, but any movement felt like too much. Half bent over on the ground, I replied, "Think I'll just sit the rest out."

I stumbled off the field, then stumbled all the way to my dorm and collapsed on the bed. The rooms were intended for four, but by some stroke of luck, I'd landed a private room.

I spent the remainder of the evening either sweating profusely or shivering uncontrollably, and between the bouts of hot and cold, vomiting like I'd never vomited before.

I woke early the next morning in a bed saturated with cold sweat. My plan had been to visit my mother in Janesville, Wisconsin, after the camp. Seeing as her house was only ninety minutes away, compared to the four hours to Eau Claire, I saw no reason to change plans. I could have used some motherly TLC.

No other staff were awake. I left a scribbled note apologizing for my sudden departure tacked to Cliff's door and headed to my car. My first stop was to find the nearest fast-food restaurant for a 7-Up to sip while I maneuvered northwest to Janesville.

Ninety minutes and one well-chewed straw later, I pulled up to my mother's quaint brick house. Mom met me at her exterior kitchen door, brown curls held back with a floral scarf. The smile fell from her face as she took in the sight of me.

She held a tan hand up to my forehead, then turned to shout into the house, "Don—you need to take Scott to the emergency room."

Two

BETWEEN A MEMORY AND A DREAM

To borrow a line from "You Don't Know How It Feels" by Tom Petty, "I woke up in between a memory and a dream." The last thing I remember is the anxious look on my mother's face as she watched my stepfather drive me to the ER. She held her hands clasped in front of her, as if resisting the urge to reach out. Her lavender dress matched the lilies in the yard. It would be the last time I saw her for a month. Somewhere beneath the nausea and fatigue was the urge to tell her everything would be fine, but I think even then a part of me thought it wouldn't be. This wasn't heat exhaustion. It wasn't the flu or food poisoning. It was something else—something far worse.

I was lying in a tiny hospital room packed with every type of medical machine known to man—a sight I could only see with my peripheral vision because of the neck brace I found myself in. The largest machine housed a beige accordion that rose and fell in time with my breathing. From it snaked a long white tube over the bedrail, across my shoulder, up to my face, and into my mouth.

There was a tube shoved down my throat.

A tube. In my throat.

Don't be afraid, my morphine-laced mind told me soothingly. *This is clearly a dream.* I tried to gag, but my body seemed to have forgotten how. I couldn't move anything. I tried to lift my arm, but nothing happened. I told my leg to kick, to flail, to lift, to do something—but got nothing. *Was I in a full body brace? What kind of dream is this?*

Out of the corner of my eye, I could see people in green uniforms hurrying past the glass-paneled wall to my left. Greeting cards covered the wall across from my bed. Colorful Mylar balloons emblazoned with cheery *Get Well!* messages sagged on their strings.

"Scott."

A woman's voice. I tore my gaze from the balloons to find her. She stood with her back to me just beyond the machines. Her brown ponytail contrasted nicely with the hunter green of her hospital scrubs. She said my name so familiarly, as if she'd used it a hundred times before.

"You really need to see this," she said. From my position in the bed, the army of machines blocked whatever she was looking at. I could hear women's voices cheering and shouting and guessed that she was watching a television screen. I wasn't sure I'd ever been in a dream with a TV—or a dream with a tube shoved down my throat, for that matter.

The woman turned toward me. Our eyes locked. I definitely didn't recognize her. For a moment, she went completely still. I stared at her, half-waiting for her to pull a Linda Blair on me or some other supernatural dream magic trick. What I got was super-natural calm.

"Good afternoon, Scott," she said. Her voice was smooth and soft, as if there were nothing at all amiss. "You've been asleep quite a while." A smile started pulling at her mouth. It grew until it became almost giddy in its exuberance.

"I'll be right back," she said, then spun and hurried from the room.

Wait— I tried to call out to her, but the tube lodged in my insides turned my cry into a muffled groan. Sweat started beading on my forehead. *I'm ready to wake up now. For real this time.*

I didn't recognize the face of the man who came into my room next, several minutes later. But his white lab coat and pressed sky-blue shirt spelled doctor. I focused on the somber line of his mouth and his narrow-set brown eyes, studying his face as if it held a clue as to why I was here. It was slowly dawning on me that this—despite the surreal horrors surrounding me—was no dream. I was really in a hospital, really gagged and neck-braced. And I really couldn't move.

The man bent at the waist to bring his face comfortably into my view and leaned toward me. "Hi, Scott," he said, putting his hand on my shoulder. "I'm Dr. Henrickson. You've been very sick and had all of us quite worried." By the look in his eyes, this wasn't just a line. They really had been worried about me.

"You've made it down a very long road. The tube in your throat is providing you with air and is connected to this machine." He gestured to the blue, Star-Trekian monstrosity with the accordion inside it.

"The other machines have been necessary to keep you alive and may remain so for a little while longer. The ones you can't see are the pulse oximeter, which has been monitoring the oxygenation of your blood; an intravenous drip to keep you hydrated; and the dialysis machine, which has been taking the place of your kidneys."

I felt my mind rock and sway the way it might moments before sleep. *Pulse oximeter. Intravenous drip. Dialysis. Keep me alive?* Even I knew these machines were used when a patient was in bad shape—really bad shape. *What I didn't know was why that patient was me. What the hell happened to me?*

On cue, Dr. Henrickson said, "I want to tell you about why you're here and why you're bandaged."

Are the bandages what's keeping me from moving? Did they strap me down to the bed? Panic rose another notch. I could only turn my head an inch to either side and could see nothing below the blue tube in my mouth, which I was purposely avoiding focusing on. *I refuse to think of the worst ... paralysis. No. Bandages mean external—not internal—damage.* I stared wide-eyed at Dr. Henrickson's brown eyes, counting my breaths.

"You contracted a serious illness, Scott. One which nearly killed you," Dr. Henrickson said. "We refer to it as toxic shock syndrome. You may have heard the media refer to it as the flesh-eating disease."

My eyes grew wider. I strained against the neck brace. Images of microscopic insects eating my skin filled my mind—*Get them off, get them off, get them off!*

"The official name is Group A Streptococcus, G-A-S for short," Dr. Henrickson said. "It's most commonly recognized as the cause of strep throat and impetigo. But in its invasive form, it's also caused scarlet and rheumatic fever—and necrotizing fasciitis."

He paused. "Which is where the flesh-eating component comes in." This time he at least had the decency to wince slightly at the words *flesh-eating.* Or maybe he was just wincing at my aghast expression.

He went on. "You see, in the throat or on the skin, the bacteria can reside unnoticed or with only mild symptoms and discomfort. But in rare cases such as yours, it's able to infect the blood, muscle, fat tissue, or lungs. When this happens, it can rapidly become life-threatening."

He paused again. Was he waiting for a response? Or was he just letting the information soak in? *If I could have covered my ears and hummed—I can't hear you, I can't hear you!—I would have.* As it was, the "lifesaving" machines that surrounded me held me captive.

"As the disease progressed, your system went into multiple organ failure and shock. We were forced to put you on full life support in a medically induced coma. You've been in that coma for the past month."

The last date I remembered was July 11—the day after the Nike camp. One month later ... *it must be mid-August.* We were supposed to arrive in Europe in late July. *I hope they still went.*

"During your coma, the necrotizing fasciitis caused the skin on your hands and feet to become gangrenous. To prevent it from spreading and eventually killing you, we had to amputate."

I stopped the fast-running train of thoughts about the Holland Cup in Europe. *Did he just say amputate?* We locked eyes. I asked him with my pleading stare, *Amputate what?*

Dr. Henrickson pursed his mouth and glanced away. I wanted to grab him by the shoulders and shake him. *AMPUTATE WHAT?*

When he met my frightened gaze again, he looked about as happy to be there as I was. "We ... were forced to remove your hands up to your mid-forearms and the front part of both your feet."

I started to laugh. Or at least I thought I was, but the life support prevented me. *You didn't cut off my hands and feet—who does this guy think he is, Al Capone? This isn't a mafia movie, and I'm not a fucking quadruple amputee.*

As if sensing he was losing his audience, Dr. Henrickson said, "Scott, I know it's hard to accept these things right now, but you have to understand: if we hadn't done the surgeries, you never would have survived. The disease would have killed you. I think you only did survive because you're a fighter and you were in excellent physical condition.

"Your muscles are severely atrophied, which is why you find it hard to move now. But you're past the most difficult part. Now you just need to heal."

He squeezed my shoulder and straightened to a standing position. His lab coat swished behind him as he turned to look over the machines at my bedside. He checked this, tapped that, and jotted a few things down on a clipboard before turning back to me.

Laying his hand on my shoulder once more, he said, "Your mother and stepfather should be here soon." With two last good-luck pats, he told me to rest and disappeared into the abyss of movement outside.

I followed him with my eyes until he was too far down the

hallway. My gaze shifted hazily to the wall opposite my bed, filled with dozens and dozens of cards and handwritten notes. I stopped counting at thirty. *I guess people know where I am.*

A month, Dr. Henrickson had said. *I'd been in the hospital, in this bed, in a coma, for a month.* I couldn't process it at all. *I didn't want to process it. This was not how my life was supposed to go. I had done everything I was supposed to do. I'd followed all the rules for a good life. I'd worked hard, eaten right, exercised regularly. I'd been good.*

I felt a tear fall onto my face and instinctively went to wipe it away. But, of course, my arm didn't move. Either way, I didn't have any hands left to wipe my face.

Three

A MOTHER'S ULTIMATUM

It was still light out when I was pulled from sleep by a gentle hand on my shoulder and a soft voice calling my name. I peered through slit eyes at my surroundings to find my family standing around me.

Mom's face came into view above me. A brown curl fell across her brow as she bent to kiss my forehead. Beside her, Don stood with his thumbs wedged in his suspenders. On my other side, my older sister Nancy leaned against her husband, Jim.

My eyes swept giddily across their faces like a kid in a candy store, trying desperately to soak everything in. *You have no idea how glad I am to see you,* I thought as Mom stroked my hair. I pretended not to notice the tremble in her hand. I turned to Jim's grinning face instead; he was smiling, but his eyes were tired and wary. *Man, he looks stiffer than me.*

Maybe it was the vice grip Nancy had on his forearm.

I sought frantically for a way to lighten the mood. In situations like this, I was usually the comic relief, armed to the teeth with sarcastic quips. But now, when my humor was needed most, I could use none of it. *How do you make a joke when the only thing you can move is your eyelids?* If I started blinking fanatically, they'd probably think I was having a seizure.

I wanted to bite down on the damn tube in my throat—to grind it to tiny, unidentifiable fragments and spout, *Hey, I'm okay! Really!* I had woken from the coma and lived through the flesh-eating disease, but I couldn't offer a single word of solace to my family.

I turned my gaze to the ceiling in frustration.

"You're not looking so good," Jim dad-joked.

Nancy shot him a narrow-eyed look of disapproval, but I appreciated his smart-ass comment—his attempt to lighten the mood and bridge the chasm between us all.

I still look better than you, old man. I sent him a silent thank-you for the effort and for the years of having my back.

Mom feigned disapproval, too, but even she couldn't hide her smile. At last, it seemed the atmosphere in the room was lightening, slowly. My family was no longer standing by my deathbed, ready to say their goodbyes, marinating for weeks in the impending loss that had awaited them.

Nancy gave me a kiss and her signature big-sister smile—a doting mix of compassion, protectiveness, and authoritative disapproval of a little brother who just can't get anything right. *I loved that smile.*

Before anyone could say more, the nurse from earlier stepped into the room. I watched her move to the end of my bed, smiling at everyone clustered around me.

"How're we all doing in here?" she asked. After a short-lived round of half-meant courtesies, she turned to me. "I don't think we've been formally introduced, Scott. I'm Lindy."

Motion from my right drew my attention. I glanced over in time to see Mom ducking out of sight, a trembling hand raised to her brow. I could only imagine how the weeks of the coma had worn on her. I would have given anything in that moment to reassure her.

"You look like a man who is well-loved," Lindy continued,

turning to my family. "Did you all hear that the key to pulling Scott out of the coma was a bunch of lanky women in bikinis?"

"What's that now?" Don asked.

"It's true," she said. "I had ESPN on, as always, and they were airing a women's beach volleyball tournament. I think I even said something to Scott about how he was missing out and needed to see the show. Then I turned around, and what do you know? His eyes were wide open! If I had known all he was waiting for were some girls to show a little skin, I'd have tuned it to something other than ESPN long ago."

Just as everyone was beginning to slacken their reserve, Dr. Henrickson strode into the room. He took up his post at the foot of my bed. A surge of dread coursed through me.

"Hello, everyone," he said, surveying our small crowd. "I thought now would be a good time to lay out the plan for the next few days while you're all in attendance."

Like a well-trained militia, everyone came to attention at Dr. Henrickson's summons. They were eager to hear what was in store for my future—as was I. *Does he know I have a soccer program to get back to? Preseason training is starting soon.*

"First," Dr. Henrickson began, "I anticipate the intubation tube to be removed sometime tomorrow morning. Your kidneys seem to be in good shape, Scott. We're going to do a few more days of dialysis treatments with the expectation that you'll be producing urine on your own afterward. If that's the case, you'll have made it past the renal failure."

"So, he's not sick anymore?" Mom asked.

"He's out of the woods in terms of the infection," Dr. Henrickson said. "The next step is to focus on getting Scott strong enough to transfer to the rehabilitation unit."

Turning to me, he added, "This isn't going to be easy ... by any stretch of the imagination. Your muscles are severely atrophied. You've dropped forty pounds, mostly muscle. You'll need to rebuild what you've lost."

"How long do you estimate before he can be transferred to rehab?" Mom asked. She was watching Dr. Henrickson with frightening intensity, her eyes alight with a determination I knew all too well.

"Two to three weeks, typically. But with the right patient, sooner."

I met the doctor's eyes and held them. His meaning was clear: a challenge had been issued, and I had every intention of rising to the occasion. *I've been in this godforsaken bed long enough. The sooner I can place myself cleanly on the road to recovery, the better—for everyone.*

"I'm sorry to send you all away so soon," Dr. Henrickson said, "but Scott does need to rest. You're welcome to return tomorrow, of course."

Lindy and Dr. Henrickson cleared out to give my family and me a moment of privacy. They took turns patting and kissing me and telling me how glad they were to see me awake (even if I looked god-awful, as Jim lovingly informed me I did).

Jim, Nancy, and Don filed out of my room, but Mom hung back. She rested one hand on the rail of my bed and turned to look at them.

"I'll be there in a minute."

Knowing better than to dispute her, they continued into the hall, drifting out of sight and earshot.

Mom leaned into my line of view just as Dr. Henrickson had done earlier that morning. Locked in the crosshairs of her sight, I forgot the tubes and machines. I forgot everything except my ball-buster of a mother squaring off with me.

Before she turned twenty, my mom was already a war widow with a newborn son—my oldest brother, Denny. She'd married her high school sweetheart at seventeen, then waved goodbye to him five months later when he went to Europe as a U.S. Army paratrooper in World War II. He came home just once, on leave, then never again. Mom was left without a husband to raise a son without a father.

Years later, she married the man who would become my father, and together they had five more children: Nancy, Rick, Jeff, yours truly, and my baby sister, Lisa.

My dad was not an easy man to live with. When the abuse became too much, Mom filed for divorce—something nearly unheard of at the time. In the sixties, women were expected to shut up and suck it up at home. But that wasn't Mom's style. She raised all six of us single-handedly while juggling three jobs and her role as president of the Wisconsin Chapter of the League of Women Voters. I never asked how she kept herself moving forward, but I've always known that it was from my mother that I inherited my positive attitude and strong work ethic. And my stubbornness.

As a product of the sixties, the most influential person in my life growing up—aside from my mother—was Walter Cronkite. Every night, I lay on my stomach, chin in hands, in front of the console television on the carpeted floor of our living room as the announcer proclaimed, *"From CBS News Headquarters in New York, this is the CBS Evening News with Walter Cronkite."* Against the sound of the ticker-tape machine in the background, Cronkite shuffled his papers and got straight into the news of the day. Through him, I experienced the Civil Rights Movement and the emergence of Martin Luther King Jr. Cronkite was my guide to the war in Vietnam and the protests against it at home. He was the one who told me about the assassinations of King and Robert Kennedy—moments that taught me to begin questioning humanity.

I once read that, as adults, we are what we were as children. It's in our childhood that our foundation is formed. The rest of our life is used to build the structure on top of that foundation— the design and strength of which are up to us.

Mom wrapped her hand around the hospital bedrail. "It doesn't matter what anyone else thinks is or is not possible, Scott," she said. "You're going to work hard and figure out ways to move forward."

The commander in chief had issued her order. This was no

time for messing around—I had my work cut out for me. She was going to see to it that I didn't slack off.

I lowered my eyelids once with slow deliberation. *No arguments here, Mom.*

She nodded, kissed me on the forehead, and strode from the room with her head held high, her shoulders a tight line beneath her bright floral dress. My mom could still take me down a peg, even as a thirty-five-year-old grown man.

As I closed my eyes to rest, I wondered how much of her strength had rubbed off on me over the years. Hopefully a lot. I had a feeling I'd be needing all I could get.

Four

IN THE HEAT OF THE NIGHT

The next time I opened my eyes, day had turned to night. I felt like I was lying under a heat lamp. My face was sweltering, my body seemingly suffocating under the weight of the blankets. Blood pulsed behind my ears, gushing in a searing torrent through my skull. A sheen of sweat broke out across my forehead.

My instinct was to throw the covers off, but instincts are useless when you're paralyzed by atrophied muscles. The blankets felt overpowering. The room was scorching. There wasn't enough air. I felt like I couldn't breathe; it was so hot. The beeping of the machines increased in pace, blurring into one endless, high-pitched scream.

I need to cool off, I need to move, I thought to myself.

My eyes flew to the glass wall. Nothing moved beyond the confines of my room. No people walking briskly about the nurses' station. No visitors wandering in or out of loved ones' rooms. No sign of life.

I was alone. *I needed to get someone's attention.*

There had to be a call button somewhere close by—every hospital room had one, didn't they? *Where the hell is it?* I begged.

It has to be here.

I scanned the room frantically. So many devices, but none of them looked right. Then I spotted it: a gadget shaped like a TV remote hanging just to the right of my jaw, with a big blue button in the middle. All I had to do was lift my arm to face height and press the button. No great feat, nothing to think twice over. *Just raise your arm,* I thought, coaching myself. *Lift it that small, tiny amount, and you'll be okay.*

I focused, thinking about motion, imagining action. The serratus anterior muscle lifts the arm above the horizontal plane. Bicep contracts to lift forearm. Anterior deltoid takes over, raising arm forward and upward. I had made this motion countless times throughout my life. I could certainly manage it once more. Right?

Raise, curl, lift. Raise. Curl. Lift.

My arm twitched, a fraction of movement upwards, but remained mostly as it was: a useless stump at my side. The call button hung tauntingly out of reach.

Maybe if I could just turn my head to the side, I could press it with my chin. I strained against the head guard.

So close. I just had to move a few inches. *Let me move!*

My head remained trapped. I was trapped. Immobilized by my disease and the apparatuses trying to save me from it. Terror, deadly and cruel, crept over me. It slithered into my consciousness inch by inch, swallowing rational thought. My heart pounded against my ribs. I began to feel light-headed. I wanted to weep. I wanted to beat anything within reach. I wanted to scream.

"AAAAAAAAAAAHHHHHHHH!" I yelled and yelled into the intubation tube. I screamed with all my might, forcing my terror, desperation, and frustration into the tube—but no sound came out. I had nothing left. I was buried alive.

After what felt like a lifetime, a nurse passed my room. By some grace of God, she paused by my door and looked into the room. She watched me for a moment, oblivious to my screams, but sensing that something was wrong. Maybe the frantic beeping of the machines gave me away.

She strode into my room, not bothering to turn on the lights.

Help! Get me out of here! Let me out! I cried within myself.

She walked around my bed to the right side near the machines and said, "What's wrong, Scott?"

I'm burning—it's too hot in here. Please. Turn it off. Turn off the heat. Please! I can't breathe.

"Everything's okay. Shh," she said. She began stroking my hair. Her voice was exaggeratedly calm, the tone you use when dealing with a frightened animal.

"Scott, I want to help you, so I'm going to ask you some questions, okay? Blink once if the answer is yes, twice for no. Do you understand?"

Blink.

"Okay. Are you in physical pain?" Blink. Blink.

"Do you feel pain in your hands or feet?" Blink. Blink.

"Are you scared?" Blink.

"It's okay to be scared." I stared at her, unblinking.

"All right. Are you feeling sick?" Blink. Blink.

"Are you too hot?"

Blink.

Blink.

Blink.

"Okay. Let's get you cooled off and see if that helps. Sound good?"

Blink.

She reached across me and tugged the covers down, rolling them at the foot of the bed. I watched, anticipating a soothing gust of cool air. No such rush came. My eyes shot to the nurse as she returned to head-level.

It's still hot. Please, make it stop. I tried desperately to convey my discomfort.

She rubbed a hand across my forehead and hair, nodding as if she understood. "All right, Scott. I'm going to step out and find a nice cool towel to help bring your temperature down. Will you be okay if I leave you here alone for a moment?"

Blink.

Relax, I told myself as I watched her leave. *She's coming back. You're not going to die.*

Just chill out.

Slowly, I heard the machine beeps slow down, my heart rate finally returning to normal. But the heat still pressed down on me like a massive vehicle compactor. Moments later, the nurse returned carrying a bin of water and a white towel. She dipped the towel in the water and wrung it out once before placing it across my forehead. It wasn't audible, but I sighed a deeply gratifying release of air.

We fell into a rhythm: she dipped the towel, wrung it out, laid it across my forehead momentarily, then dabbed it about the accessible parts of my face and neck. I watched her dip and wring from the corner of my eye, then followed the motion of the towel like a dog watching its treat descend into mouth-reach.

"Better?" she asked.

Blink.

She patted my face with the towel one last time before letting it fall back into the basin. She tuned the television to CNN Headline News. "I'll check back in on you in half an hour, all right?"

Blink.

Alone again. It was strange how someone accustomed to independence and living on his own could so quickly come to crave the company of others.

So, this was my life: trapped in a world of total dependence. No matter how hard I worked, I was forever altered. I had no hands. No feet, basically. I couldn't scratch my own nose, let alone stand up.

Never had I felt so vulnerable. I could've died in that hospital bed before anyone even realized something was amiss. It felt wrong to have survived these past weeks, fighting off infections and battling a deadly bacterium, only to lose everything in the cover of night. I was too young to be reduced to this.

I didn't even know if I'd be able to run again. Or dribble a ball down a soccer field. The thought of never playing soccer again was unbearable. Like the death of a loved one. This was more than the loss of parts of my limbs; this was the loss of the love of my life, my sole ambition since I was a teenager. My identity.

Playing soccer was my greatest form of expression. It was my art. With a ball as my brush and the blank canvas of a soccer field, I could funnel my emotions into the creation of my design and leave them on the field when I was done.

But you can still teach, the optimistic part of my mind reminded me. *You have a college soccer program. Don't forget that.*

There was no going back now. Obviously. My hands and feet had already been taken from me. But I couldn't simply exist forever as I was now, a grown man reduced to a helpless version of what he once was. No, I had to find a way to get out of here—to remove myself from this situation and ensure it never happened again. As far as I knew, I still had a coaching position waiting for me back at UW–Eau Claire. As long as I had my work and the program, I could find a way to move forward. My greatest asset as a soccer player had always been my ability to outlast my opponent because of my training and preparation. Plus, I had my good-old Wisconsin work ethic to see me through. I just needed the training regimen.

My mom's voice drifted through my head: *You're going to work hard and figure out ways to move forward.* A lifelong marathon was ahead of me—and I hadn't even crossed the starting line.

Five

COUNTING DOWN

The removal of the intubation tube was one thing, but the catheter was something very different. Untethered from the big blue machine and the neck brace, to some extent, I felt free. But my atrophied muscles created an obstacle.

It's not impossible to exercise while lying prone in a hospital bed. As weak as I was, moving my arms and legs even slightly was a struggle. But every movement I made redeveloped my atrophied limbs. No one had told me not to exercise—and I needed something to focus on. A goal. I needed to work. Remembering many of the exercises the "Godfather of Fitness," Jack LaLanne, performed on his television show and mimicked by my mom while Jeff, Lisa, and I followed her, I practiced lifting my arms and legs, just a little, every hour. Pretty soon, I could lift them completely and hold them up in the air.

By my seventh day fully awake in intensive care, they deemed me stable enough to transfer to the rehabilitation unit. The day of my transfer, I sat with the TV off, awaiting my ride out of the ICU. My muscles were sore, but they held the kind of excitement they always had before a soccer match. I just wanted to move.

I watched the glass wall to my left like it was a stage. The people passing were the actors—nurses in hunter green, doctors in flapping white coats, families hugging the wall with uncertain expressions. Then, finally, two men in blue scrubs appeared, steering a gurney between them. My shining chariot come to transport me back to my old life. Or one step closer to it, at least.

Lindy propped the door open and ushered them in. They positioned the gurney alongside my bed. I inhaled the factory tang of the disposable sheet covering and thought of freedom. As the attendants stationed themselves at the head and foot of my bed, Lindy pulled the covers off me.

"You ready to do this, Scott?" she asked.

I took a deep breath. "More ready than you know."

One of the attendants placed a spine board on the bed beside me. They rolled me onto my side, slid the board beneath me, then laid me back down. I tried my best to keep my body stiff to make the maneuvering easier.

"One, two, three, go," the man at my head said. I was hoisted up just enough to hover over the mattress then quickly shifted onto the edge of the gurney. I used my heels and elbows to lift myself so I could scoot the rest of the way into the middle of the table unassisted, allowing the men to slide the board away without having to roll me.

"Wow!" Lindy looked down at me, impressed. "When did you learn to do that?"

"Oh, you know. Just a little something I picked up," I responded hoarsely.

Lindy smiled and shook her head. To the attendants, she said, "It's about time you get this nuisance out of my ward."

They chuckled. "Sure thing," the one by my feet said in a hup-two tone. With a tug and a push, we were off.

Lindy came up to walk alongside me. She had my case of cassette tapes and an oscillating fan cupped under her arms. Seeing her at my side carrying the only material things that mattered to me, I felt a tightness cross my chest. I had been so caught up in getting out of the ICU, it hadn't even crossed my mind what I was leaving behind. Lindy had befriended and supported my family while I was comatose, becoming almost like a second mother to me in my short conscious span in the ICU.

As they wheeled me into an elevator, I tried to find something to say that would make this parting less bitter and more sweet. But before I could find the right words, my throat seized. A memory tugged at me—one I could tell by the knot in my stomach that I didn't want back. I'd been in this elevator before, and the journey hadn't been a happy one: amputation day. The day they took my hands and feet.

In the memory, I was lying on a similar gurney, surrounded by two men and a woman in surgical scrubs and caps. Theirs were a lighter green than the ICU nurses'. I looked up as the doors slid closed by my head.

"Everything's going to be okay," the woman assured me. I wanted to trust her. These people held my future in their hands, after all. But there was still a pit of terror knotted at the base of my stomach as the numbers over the door counted down to the basement.

The elevator dinged. The doors opened. I was rolled down a white hallway. We turned through a doorway into a brightly lit room. Colorful drawers and shelves lined one wall. A stainless-steel table was center stage. Giant spotlights and other contraptions I couldn't name extended from the ceiling overhead. Eric Clapton's "Lay Down Sally" was playing faintly.

"We always play music during surgery," the female doctor told me. She shimmied her shoulders to the beat. "For you, it's *Clapton's Greatest Hits* CD."

"Feel free to skip his 'Knockin' on Heaven's Door' cover if it's on there," I said as they transferred me onto the operating table. It was cold and hard beneath me.

Surgical masks were pulled over faces. I, too, received a mask, though mine wasn't made of cloth. I started to lift a hand to stop them—but I stopped myself, curled my fingers into as tight a fist as I could muster, and inhaled deeply.

"Scott," one of the masked faces said from somewhere above me, "can you count backward from a hundred for me?"

I tried to pick the face of the man who had spoken out of the crowd, but my vision was already beginning to blur. I blinked and breathed and began to count down to the sounds of Clapton's greatest hits.

"One hundred ..."

"I long to see the morning light ..."

"Ninety-nine ... Ninety-eight ..."

"Coloring your face so dreamily ..."

"Ninety-seven ... Ninety-six ..."

"So don't you go and say goodbye ..."

"Ninety ... five ..."

"You can lay your worries down and stay with me ..."

"Ninety ... four ..."

"And don't you ever leave ..."

The chime of the elevator jerked me from my memory. A lump had formed in my throat. I tried to swallow it, but my mouth was too dry. *It's strange,* I thought—*I was awake on amputation day. I know I was awake.*

I must have known what was coming. I'd been fully aware of the impending surgeries. Had I agreed to let them amputate? It seemed I must have. I had agreed to the amputations, to this disfigured life. Me. My choice. *Why would I do that to myself?*

Shortly after I was settled in my room in the rehab facility, a white-coated doctor appeared in my doorway. His dark brown hair was neatly combed, and a two-day-old beard shaded the lower half of his face. I gave him a quick once-over, silently commending his Dockers. I always wore Dockers, a pressed shirt, and tie on match days.

"Hey there, Scott," he said as he walked the rest of the way into my room. "I'm Dr. Molin, the head honcho here in rehab. Mind if I chat with you for a bit?"

"By all means," I said. He looked around my room with his hands clasped behind his back as if it weren't just like any other room on this floor. He sauntered over to my collection of music in the corner and idly began flipping through the cassettes, taking a few out to scan their front and back covers.

"So. Rehab," he said, still looking down at the tapes. Seemingly as an afterthought, he glanced up and smiled at me. "Welcome."

"Thanks."

He went back to perusing the music. "The goal of rehab is to prepare you for prostheses to be fitted, to learn how to use them competently, and, ultimately, to get the hell out of here." He paused. "Is this a Jackson Browne tape I see?" He laughed to himself, holding the recording up so I could see its cover.

"Sure is. You a fan?"

"Yeah, I am." He paused again. "So, you were an athlete before coming here, right?"

I nodded, wincing at his use of past tense. *I was. I'm not anymore.*

"Good, then you should have no problem accepting a training regimen. But you may be bored—oh, look at that!" He gestured at another cassette in his hands. "You've got Steve Miller and Boz Scaggs in here, too. Very nice."

He turned toward me. "So, what injuries have you had and rehabilitated from in the past?"

"As a teen, I had two knee surgeries—one from football and the other from baseball injuries."

"Well, that's good. You've been around the block, so you

know the drill pretty well. This'll be like recovering from your knee surgeries except longer and harder. Think you can handle it?"

"Yup."

"Now wait a minute." He withdrew another case from my box. "What is a white boy from Wis-*cahn*-sin doing with funk music?" He exaggerated the slow drawl of Wisconsin in a mockery of the Midwest. "Are you lost, white boy? Look at this!" He marveled. "You got Sly and the Family Stone and The Isley Brothers, too. Your compass is definitely off."

"I love funk. There aren't many of us, but some Wis-*cahn*-sinites do have taste."

"Could've fooled me. You may be the hippest Wisconsinite I've ever met."

Finally abandoning my music collection, he walked over to the foot of my bed. He crossed his arms. "Now, Scott, how are you handling the amputations?"

His quick change in tone brought me up short. I was still busy playing mental cat and mouse and looking for the joke—until his words registered. I realized the game was over. I let my smile slide into a straight line.

"Scott, you're disabled. And pretty bad, too."

I looked down at my body. My arms ended a foot too soon in thick layers of white gauze. The blankets sagged at the ends of my feet where my toes should have been sticking up. I didn't need reminding of my disability. I couldn't forget if I tried.

"It's okay if there are days you don't want to work or speak with anyone," Dr. Molin said. He paused, allowing the words to sink in. I looked up at him. Was he expecting me to add to this part of the conversation? I'd rather go back to talking about funk music.

Dr. Molin held my gaze. "Time keeps on slippin', slippin', slippin' into the future ..."

"'Fly Like an Eagle,'" I chirped.

He smiled. "You'll need to come to terms with that, and the

sooner you accept the prosthetics, the sooner you'll move forward."

We stared at each other for a few breaths. I glanced away first. From the corner of my eye, I saw Dr. Molin nod to himself and turn to leave.

He paused halfway to the door and turned back around. "Do you like bagels?"

I frowned. *What's this guy getting at? First, he chats about music and jokes around, then he reminds me just how bad my new life is, and now he wants to talk about my taste in food?*

"Uh, sure?" I replied.

"Good." He marched through the door. No explanation, no follow-up, no uplifting pep talk.

Welcome to rehab.

Six

A HARSH REALITY

The next day, about an hour after my first gourmet hospital-issue breakfast in rehab, a dainty woman with a ponytail of golden hair flying out behind her came twirling into my room.

She was literally twirling. I watched, amazed, as she spun again and again, dancing over toward my bed. She slowed her rotation as she drew near, spinning around one final time before coming to a standstill in front of me. When the dizzying blur had stilled into the form of a solid person, I recognized the beaming smile of my occupational therapist.

Kathy looked at me with her twinkling brown eyes, clapped her hands, and sang out, "Time to get to work!"

She walked over to where the bed controls were and held the "up" button, humming to herself as she waited for the bed to carry me to her desired height. Kathy was ... eccentric. But she was also my coach. Once I had my wits about me, I found that any remnants of sleepiness had been yanked away by her performance like an old Band-Aid, gone before you even knew it was going.

When the head of my bed was at a forty-five-degree angle,

Kathy skipped around me to lower both guard rails and pull back the tan blanket and white sheets covering my atrophied legs. I stole a glimpse of what lay in front of me: the knobby knees too big for my bony legs, the sagging flesh where hard-earned muscle once was. I quickly looked away.

Kathy reached under my thighs and calves, then carefully pulled my legs to the left, twisting my lower body so my bandaged feet stuck out over the edge of the bed. They were wrapped from calf to amputated foot, so I looked like I had no ankles—just two long, mangled peg legs.

I hated the sight of my body—the starved shapes of my limbs and cavernous feel to my abdomen juxtaposed by the bulging joints and mangled, amputated ends. *I'm going to change this,* I thought. *Kathy and I are going to change this.*

She rested her right hand on my left shoulder and met my eyes. "Ready to try sitting up without the bed for support?" Her dark eyebrows arched over wide eyes twinkling with excitement.

"Absolutely."

She wrapped her right arm around my back. "Go ahead and lean on me, Scott."

I obliged, and she began to pull me toward the edge of the bed. I used the end of my right arm to help scoot myself forward until my legs were dangling over the bed.

"Well done," she said triumphantly when I was settled, my breathing the only thing the worse for wear. "I only needed to help you balance—the rest was all you. Talk about a head start."

I smiled, glad we were doing well so soon but a little dismayed by how much effort moving those few inches had required.

"Now for the hard part: I'm going to take a step back and support only your shoulders while you sit for a full minute. Okay?"

I nodded, trying to fathom how sitting had become such a challenge. With only Kathy's meager support, I felt my body trying to cave under me. She glanced at the clock and then back to me.

Sixty seconds had never lasted so long. My abdomen burned, my back ached, and my chest heaved as the clock slowly counted down. Beads of sweat had broken out on my forehead. I had been in training for most of my life, but nothing compared to this. I became acutely aware of every place on my body where I'd lost those forty pounds of muscle.

"Four ... three ... two ... one," Kathy said. She swooped in with her arms under mine to support me. I sagged against her.

"Rest for a minute and we'll try again, all right?" I dipped my chin, biting back a whimper at the word "again."

After the sluggish progression of the previous minute, my sixty seconds of rest seemed to slip by unnoticed. Just when I thought my breathing was beginning to slow down, Kathy cleared her throat and gave my right shoulder a squeeze.

"Ready to go again?" she asked.

I swallowed and licked my lips. "Ready."

She maneuvered to the front of me again, and we began the hellish trial once more. In some ways, the subsequent sets became easier because they had lost their shock factor. I went into each of the five reps knowing that this one would be worse than the last but determined to make it through nonetheless. My abdomen was a furnace of heat and pain—*But this,* I reminded myself, *is what you wanted. You want to move. You need this pain.* I forced myself to revel in the burn of muscles rebuilding.

"Okay," Kathy breathed when the fifth set of sixty seconds had ticked by. She helped me move back against the head of the bed. I sank into the cushioned support of the mattress.

She took her time putting the bed rails back into place and lowering the bed to horizontal. I began to wonder if she was dilly-dallying so she could make sure I recovered okay. Pausing with her arm on the left handrail, she leaned on her forearm as she looked at me, pondering. I watched her eyes wander over my sweaty face and the rise and fall of my chest.

"That was such a good start ... I'm just thinking what other exercises we could add to keep you progressing as fast as possible," she said.

I grinned. "Go to the foot of the bed."

She looked at me, her brow furrowed, and opened her mouth to respond. I silenced her with a pointed nod in the direction of my feet. Shrugging, she turned and walked to where I had indicated.

"Now hold down my ankles," I told her.

At this, her expression opened in surprise. "You want to try a sit-up?"

I could see the head-shaking about to commence, so I quipped, "Shut up and get to work."

She blinked owlishly, then laughed and took hold of each of my ankles with a broad grin on her face. A confidence was growing between us, one that would only get stronger from here.

With her hands wrapped securely around my ankles, I reeled off ten sit-ups at a forty-five-degree angle. I pushed a gust of air out of my lungs on each upward heave. If my abdomen had been in agony before, there were no words for how it felt now. By the third sit-up, I wanted nothing more than to collapse. By six, I would have let them move me back into the ICU and reattach me to the morphine drip—but this time, more like a gas nozzle to a car. By nine, I wasn't sure I had legs anymore because I could feel nothing below my stomach. By ten, I was satisfied.

I collapsed back against the mattress, letting out a groan so loud I wouldn't have been surprised if everyone in the unit thought I'd just orgasmed. I closed my eyes and focused on the burning in my abdominals. Never in my life had an exercise rendered me this exhausted. When I opened my eyes, Kathy was still standing at the foot of my bed.

"I'm impressed," she said. "I think this is the beginning of a beautiful friendship."

"Of all the gin joints in all the towns in all the world, she walks into mine," I quoted in return.

"Humphrey Bogart. Well done. I'll be back after lunch, so get ready for more pain at my unyielding command."

Before she could skip from my room, I called out, "Hey, Kathy? What's up with Dr. Molin and bagels?"

"Every month, he has them flown in overnight from New York for the rehab staff. He's a New Yorker, through and through. If he mentioned bagels to you, he must like you." She jiggled her eyebrows and winked at me as if we were a couple of girlfriends sharing a secret.

I laughed and jerked my chin toward the door.

"Funny. Now get the hell out of my room. I need my beauty rest."

With a sigh, I leaned back to bask in my new accomplishments. I could now sit up without assistance for five nonconsecutive minutes. I'd achieved the physical fitness level of a toddler. *Go, me!*

Things quickly fell into a routine in rehab. I was visited twice a day by both Kathy and Helen, my physical therapist, and reveled in my rapid signs of improvement. For the next two weeks, Kathy continued to push me, and Helen brought bigger and bigger weights. I added crunches to my private training regimen. My strength was increasing even faster than my amputations were healing. Barely two weeks into rehab, I advanced from using the Velcro weights strapped to my arms and legs to using the Nautilus weight-training machine down the hall.

As my physical strength returned bit by bit, so too did my old cocky self. With each additional repetition and pound of weight I lifted, I felt more and more like the old me. But as I often told my players, cocky is good; arrogance is bad. And my cockiness was bordering on arrogance. My self-confidence would prove to be nothing more than a façade hiding the true injuries yet to heal.

It was sometime after breakfast and before my morning training with Kathy and Helen that Dr. Molin came into my room.

"Hey, Doc!" I called out in greeting. Just as my reputation

among the staff had progressed, my relationship with Dr. Molin had developed into a sort of brotherhood. We spoke regularly and freely, and I greatly appreciated his candor. When turbulence was ahead, I could always count on Doc Molin to keep me abreast. This morning would prove no different.

"What's happenin'?" he replied, walking to my bedside and cuffing me not-so-gently on the shoulder. I grinned and rolled my shoulder into his grip to reduce the impact.

"Eh, you know, just the usual excitement: reading the *USA Today* from front to back, flipping through channels on the TV —both via the ingenuity of holding a pencil in my mouth and using the eraser to turn the pages and press the buttons. Nothing really new."

Chuckling, he reached for my left arm. Slowly, he rotated it, studying the ace bandage wrapped around its end. After a moment of contemplation, he set my arm back on the bed. "Well, how about we take these bandages off? Is that new enough for you?"

"What, you mean remove them for good?" I had been through a few bandage changes since entering rehab. For the most part, it had become just another part of the routine.

He nodded.

I raised my eyebrows, surprised. "Sure, I could use a good scratch under there."

He smirked. But as he began removing first the white tape securing the ace bandage, then the bandage itself, and finally the gauze underneath, the smile slowly faded. We were both quiet as he exposed the ends of my arms. I was afraid. Maybe he was afraid for me.

This was it—the last time my arms would be bandaged. Before, every time they'd been removed for cleaning and inspection, it had been like watching a car wreck unfold—dreading to look because I didn't want the images of my crippled, unhealed arms in my mind but unable to turn away. *Maybe if I just don't look directly at it, the shock won't hurt so bad.*

But it did hurt. Seeing my arms—what was left of them—

shook me into disbelief. Somehow, even though I knew half of each forearm and both of my hands were gone, not seeing them in their entirety had been a sort of security blanket. It was as if nothing was set in stone. I still had to heal, and maybe once the healing was done, they would look better—less like discolored stumps and more like arms.

Each time my arms had been re-bandaged, I sighed with relief. I could file these new mental pictures in the "deal with it later" box and tuck it back into the recesses of my mind. But this time was different. I was being left with my arms, marred and fully exposed. No more palliative fantasies about miraculous healing. This was reality, finite and irrevocable.

Dr. Molin uncovered the left arm first. Underneath the tape, bandage, and gauze was my limb, cleanly severed at the middle of my forearm. The end was smooth and well-mended. I lifted it toward my face and forced my unwilling eyes to focus on it. My skin was back to its normal beige, no longer bluish-black or nause-ating yellow, and the sutures were gone, leaving a smooth white seam in their place.

Dr. Molin dropped the ball of used gauze and bandage at the end of my bed as he walked to my other side. My right arm was half an inch shorter than my left, and its end wasn't sewn together as tightly. As he unwrapped it, I swallowed the bile rising in my throat and studied the excess skin puckering at the end of my arm. Lifting it as I had the other, I brought the wound to eye level and stared at it, studying the ridges and crinkled skin of scar tissue. I was revolted. I could feel my subconscious trying to block out the image.

Hideous.

"Everything's healed nicely," Dr. Molin said, his voice calling to me from somewhere far off. I let my arms fall back to the sheets and closed my eyes.

"Judging by the amount of muscle tissue left intact, they considered the possibility of myoelectric hands," he went on. I listened without really hearing at first. His voice came to me like an echo in the wake of my sadness.

"That's good news, Scott."

I looked at him and nodded. He wanted to instill hope for the future in me, but I was still grappling with the consequences of the past. Besides, I didn't even know what myo-whatever hands were.

"Have you heard of myoelectric hands?" he asked.

"No. Are they like the hooks?" The only things possibly more revolting than my amputations were the Captain Hook-inspired contraptions I was expected to wear over them.

"Oh—much, much better. Think Luke Skywalker after he lost his hand in *The Empire Strikes Back*. The myos use electromyography signals to control the motion of the prosthesis. Whenever you open or close your hand, for instance, electrical signals are sent through the contracted muscles of your forearms. Typically, those signals travel down your forearm to your hands to tell them what to do." He ran a hand along the length of his forearm, tracing the path of the signals he spoke of.

"The myos have specially designed sensors that can read those signals off the surface of your skin and communicate them to the electric hands. No straps or cables. And the best part is, you'd have hands instead of hooks." He paused and looked at me for a while.

An alternative to the hooks? I didn't care if I only got three of five fingers; it'd still be better than one sharp fishing tool.

"The downside is, just one of those things costs about as much as a new car."

I winced. *There goes that dream.*

"You should look into how much your insurance is willing to cover and consider it," he said. "Not everyone has this option, you know."

I nodded. It was a gift from the surgeons who'd saved my life, and I wanted to accept it. My brother Rick was an insurance agent. I'd ask him to look into making the cost of the myos acceptable to my insurance company.

A flicker of hope was beginning to take shape... and it scared me senseless.

"In the meantime, the prosthetist will be by tomorrow to cast you for the hooks," he said, blowing the flicker out before it could become a flame.

Gathering up the bandages, Dr. Molin said, "Stay strong, man," then left me to my thoughts.

Seven

THE BANE OF CAPTAIN HOOK

The day the hooks arrived came much too soon. I didn't want the hooks—or the reality they signified. Even with the potential of the myos down the road, I couldn't come to terms with the fact that I needed prosthetics at all. I would be one of those people. Part human, part robot. The people you'd lie to and say you hadn't even noticed their prosthetic hand or missing leg while inside it was all you could focus on. No one liked to face reality when it came to prosthetics, because the reality was it could happen to anyone. And it happened to me.

The prosthetist was an older man who had clearly moved past the emotional side of his job long before meeting me. I first met him two weeks prior when he cast me for what would temporarily (I hoped) function as my hands.

"Good morning, Scott," he said, his voice breathy and bland. I tried to swallow the loathing that was overtaking my mood. It was unfair to hate the messenger, I knew, but I had to direct my anger somewhere. And this particular messenger came bearing the future bane of my existence.

He laid the hooks at my feet. I wanted to kick them to the

floor. I stared them down, studying the cylindrical tubes that would be my new forearms and the shiny claws that would be my new hands. My heart sank into my stomach.

"Do you have a T-shirt with you?" he asked. I motioned to the small closet to my left. "Go ahead and remove the hospital gown above your waist and put this on for me, Scott."

He held up the freshly washed, royal-blue Nike tee I'd been wearing the day I began feeling sick. I didn't even know the Scott who had worn that shirt anymore—the Scott who had led such a carefree, happy life, whose career was on track and whose biggest concern was where he'd get his next crew of new recruits. What I wouldn't give to have some of his blissful invincibility with me now.

I shrugged my arms out of the hospital gown, letting the top portion of it fall to my lap. He held the shirt out for me to take. When I didn't reach for it as he'd expected, he saw his error. A pink blush appeared on his face. He brought the shirt to me and laid it face down on my lap. It was the first time I had tried to dress without assistance, but I wasn't about to share that fact with him.

I carefully slipped my arms into the sleeves, lifted the shirt over my head, and let it slide over my face. On any other day since I arrived in rehab, this feat would have been met with a surge of pride. Today, I simply gazed blankly at the prosthetist, waiting to see what would come next.

He carried the prostheses by the wrists to my right side. Two loops of white straps were strung between them, lacing through a metal ring at the center. He placed the straps over my shoulders and across my back so that they formed an X, with the metal ring situated between my shoulder blades.

I allowed him to move me with gentle nudges while I fixated on the wall in front of me. As he held each cylindrical forearm up for me to slide my arms into, I felt like a wild horse being saddled for the first time. I wanted to rebel, jerk my arms and shoulders from his grasp, and rip the thick straps off me. I wanted to lash out, yell at him to get the hell out of my room and take his damn hooks with him. But a deeper, darker part of me held fast in the face of my fury. This darkness gradually swelled within me like a dense fog, swallowing other emotions until all that remained of me was a mindless automaton. The tighter he strapped me in, the more the fight drained out of me and the greater my numb acceptance of my fate became.

Next, he turned to the wire cables which ran along my shoulders and down the outside of each new arm. Each cable was threaded through a series of loops leading from the back of my shoulder to the outside of the prosthetic forearm. They ended at a lever at the base of the hook itself. With my arm resting comfortably at my side, elbow slightly bent, the prosthetist adjusted the cables until they were almost taut. Now I was a plow horse ready for the field.

"All right," he said when he had finished tinkering. "So, these are called body-powered prosthetic hooks because you use the motion of your shoulder to operate them. If you put tension on the cable, the hook will open." He guided me to extend my arm out in front of me. The motion of my shoulder caused the cable to pull the hook open, separating into two antennae-like apparatuses.

"Release the tension—" he had me draw my arm back toward my body so that my shoulder relaxed—"and the hook closes."

I watched it all happen with my mind shut off. I couldn't focus on or care about what he was saying.

"These rubber bands here keep them closed when there is no pull on the cable." He pointed to a thick rubber band wrapped around the base of the hook just above the joint where they opened and closed.

"You can see there are two separate hooks on each prosthesis, which allows you to grab and hold anything a hand can hold. You can also move the hooks around and lock them into various positions with this switch here." He pointed to a small sliding knob like you'd find on a flashlight.

"To take them off, first open your arms to the side to relieve the tension on the straps. Then bring your arms up and forward to draw the straps over your head. Once you're out of the harness, you can secure one prosthesis against your lap with the wrist of the other and pull your arm out of the cylinder." He smiled. "Easy!"

Unlikely. I didn't return his smile.

"Do you have any questions for me?" he asked after a pause.

"No."

"All right, then. I'll leave you to experiment. It will take some time, but many patients have had great success with these." I stared at him blankly.

"Okay. Take care, then," he said, and left.

When he had disappeared down the hall, I pulled the hooks off one at a time and fumbled them onto my bedside table. Part of my love for soccer was my ability to read a situation and evaluate it from various perspectives. It was far too easy to read the limitations the hooks would impose on my life. There was no positive way to spin it. Now that I had seen them up close, the prosthetics more closely resembled the hands of a Tyrannosaurus rex—minus the thumbs—than those of Captain Hook.

Would I be able to write? Clearly, I'd be relegated to a finger typist—or rather, a hook typist. What about driving? My five-speed manual car would most likely have to go. Tying shoes was certain to be a problem. *And that's just the beginning,* I thought. *How is this going to affect my coaching career?*

In the middle of my downward spiral, Kathy came twirling into the room. When she stopped at the foot of my bed and realized her antics hadn't raised a smile from me, she frowned. Her eyes fell on the hooks.

"So, the prosthetics arrived today. And you're not too excited about them."

"Not exactly excitement-inspiring."

"No," she said softly and rested a hand on my shin. "I guess not. But, Scott, think about how much more you'll be able to do with them that you can't do without them."

"I know, but they're so limiting. How can I do all the things I used to do with those?"

"Have you wondered at all why you feel so negatively toward the hooks?" I opened my mouth to cite some of their many limitations, but she raised a hand before I could speak. "I don't mean why you hate their limitations. This is the first time I've seen you fighting against forward progress. What is it about the hooks that's making you balk?"

I stared at her. My anger deflated like a popped balloon, leaving me with emptiness and the truth.

How have you come to know me this well? I wondered, as I looked at her, defeated. She was right: I had never turned away from progress before, especially not when that progress was a clear step up in my ability to care for myself. But these hooks were different. They were bald-faced. They were revolting.

I exhaled a long, deep sigh. "I guess it's that when I wear those hooks—or even think about wearing them—it makes me feel truly disabled. I mean, thus far my frustration has been about being dependent on others. Now all I can see are the hooks where my hands used to be." *They'll be right there,* I thought, *in my line of sight, every minute of every day.*

"Mm-hm. Well, maybe what we need is a bit of a distraction to help you focus on what the hooks can do for you rather than against you." The jovial Kathy was creeping back. I watched a delightful smile play about her lips as she said, "Don't move. I'll be right back."

She gave a little ballerina-esque leap and twirled out the door.

I smiled. I couldn't help it. When in the presence of Kathy, smiling was what you did. Even if I didn't feel fully energized, she had begun to shift my way of thinking. I could feel the tension in my shoulders lessening.

When she returned a hop, skip, and sashay later, Kathy presented me with a board about the size of two meal trays. It was adorned with various latches, buttons, zippers, snaps, and clasps one might encounter in daily life. She set the base of the board on my bedside table and leaned it back against her chest to keep it upright. She reached around to one area of the board and hooked two sections of a bra strap together.

"Let's make this realistic," she said. "Now unhook the strap."

I raised my eyebrows inquisitively at her, and she chuckled with devilish laughter.

"Hey, you never know when you'll get the opportunity."

All I could do was smile stiffly and turn to face the challenge.

Eight

WHEEL OF FORTUNE

Despite Kathy's eccentric efforts, I couldn't muster the will to eat when lunch rolled around. Nor could I energize myself enough to complete the extra sets of exercises with her and Helen in the afternoon.

By the time dinner came knocking—spaghetti and meatballs —I grimly set about the task of donning the two things I currently hated most in the world. When I had finally managed to get them on and tested that the cables were working properly, I latched my right hook onto the bedside table and wheeled it over my lap.

The savory smells of tomato sauce and meat wafted up to me, and I became suddenly very aware of just how hungry I was. It had been so long, I couldn't even picture how I once held a fork with fingers. But for the first time in two months since awakening, feeding myself was an attraction. Delicately, I rotated the right hook inward two clicks, then flexed my shoulder to open it. With the fork braced by the left hook so it wouldn't slip away, I slid the handle between the right two hooks then relaxed my shoulder. The hook closed around the utensil. Exhaling, I lifted the fork off the tray and watched as the hook held fast.

Okay, not so bad.

But to actually eat, I needed to calculate the appropriate angles of my shoulder, elbow, hook, and fork to get the food from the bowl into my mouth. Just the thought of everything that had to go into doing such an elementary task was debilitating. If my stomach hadn't been so adamant about our need for food, I'd have chucked the tray across the room.

I studied the task at hand. Like learning to drive on the opposite side of the road, I had to reorient myself to the fork and bowl. After many false starts, I finally managed to get one meager scoop of noodles into my mouth. Never had eating been such a taxing endeavor. With every misstep, it became harder to hold back my frustration—each time a spaghetti noodle landed on my lap or my fork fell onto the tray, I forced myself to take a moment to quiet the rant coursing through my mind.

By the time my mom arrived for her usual evening visit and our regular viewing of *Wheel of Fortune,* a throbbing ache had rooted itself in my skull. I tried to greet her but accidentally turned my shoulders too much and dropped the spaghetti-laden fork onto the tray.

"Shit!" I blurted. Mom flinched. Frustrated, I gritted my teeth, reoriented myself, and navigated through the seemingly never-ending process of retrieving the fork and starting again.

"Sit down, Mom," I said, my focus still on the spaghetti. I could see her poised on the end of her chair, ready to leap into the fray.

One inch at a time, I raised the forkful of noodles toward my mouth. I stretched my neck out like a turtle to make the journey shorter and wrapped my lips securely around the fork. I leaned back and turned to my mom.

"So, the hooks came today, huh?" she asked, eyeing the sauce smears and spaghetti strands clinging to the top half of my hospital gown. "How are they?"

She was trying to be casual, but her words and body language were laced with tension.

"About what you'd expect," I said, turning back to my meal. I dipped the fork into the pasta and started to lift my arm toward my mouth. Preoccupied by her and her concern for me, I miscalculated the angles, causing the fork to shoot up vertically before reaching my mouth and pasta to spill down my hook and arm.

"Oh!" Mom's hand shot out toward me.

"Don't!" I barked. She cowered back into the chair. "I'll get it," I added in a softer tone. This time I was able to bring the fork in the right direction, but halfway to my mouth, I misused my shoulder, and the hook opened. Noodles and fork tumbled onto my lap. Mom stood.

"*Let me feed myself, damn it,*" I snapped.

A whimper escaped her throat, and she turned toward the window.

"Aw, Mom—" I started to say, hating myself for hurting her.

"Why couldn't it have happened to me instead?" she blurted out.

I turned to her and froze. I watched her rounded shoulders begin to quake, and I felt sorrow that stretched far deeper than the self-pity I'd been absorbed in all day.

I wanted to say something—anything—to help her stop crying. But what words could fix this? I wished every day that this illness hadn't happened to me, but never, not once, had I wished it upon someone else instead. And never had I thought that someone I cared so deeply about would wish to take my place.

She couldn't feel responsible ... could she? This was no one's fault. It was a fluke, a random occurrence. The doctors couldn't say how the bacteria had entered my system. But now, I watched my mom consumed by a helpless misery, sobbing into the windowsill of my hospital room. I wanted to reach out to her, but I could only let my arms fall to my sides in defeat—I was confined to my bed, resigned to play audience to my mother's suffering as she had to my own.

My mother later told me how she had held vigil by my bedside during the coma. Lindy had to all but blackmail her into going home to rest my first night in intensive care. Even then, Mom only left after making Lindy promise to call the minute anything changed.

Which she did, early the next morning.

My family flocked to my bedside. Mom's pastor came for prayers. They filled my room and spilled out into the hall. The doctor told Mom that she should let me go—which, of course, she refused to do, she told me later. Instead, she began rubbing my hands where they'd begun to turn purply-black as the bacteria slowly caused my flesh to die. Maybe she could rub some life back into them, she thought. But the blackness just kept creeping up my arm, into my fingers, across my palms, over my wrists. My family watched my flesh dying inch by inch.

Nancy said she had felt an electric shock when she touched me. I was still in there, she insisted. My family didn't give up—nor did they leave. For more than a week, they slept on chairs in and around my room. Even after that, I was never alone, always accompanied by a rotating cast of sentinels. I could only imagine the suffering they had endured during the month of my coma.

Awake now, the memory of that suffering remained. There was still so much healing left to be done for all of us.

Nine

BLEEDING OUT IS COLD

I stared at her blood-splattered face. She smiled back, faintly.

How the hell did this happen?

I shook my head to clear my mind.

Amber had come to change the bandages on my feet, a routine procedure I underwent every few days. We were chatting amicably, swapping hospital gossip and news and pleasantries—then there was blood. A lot of blood. It began spraying around the room, gushing from the end of my left foot.

"I've got a bleeder!" she yelled as she clamped her hand over my foot. But the gushing didn't stop. It started squirting through the gaps in her fingers. Frantically, she grabbed the gauze she had just removed and bunched it at the top of my foot. Lines of red streaked her face, neck, and clothing. Splatters adorned the wall behind her.

I stared wide-eyed at the scene before me—blood-washed like the crime scene of a murder mystery. Amber, saturated in red, looked straight out of *Carrie*.

This can't all be coming from me, I thought. The blood was everywhere—seeping through the gauze, staining her hands, clumping in her hair, drooling down her cheek. Another nurse came sprinting into my room with Dr. Henrickson in tow, who happened to be nearby.

"Hey, Doc H," I said—or thought. I couldn't be sure which. Everything was a blur.

"Get a central line kit, Annie," he said to the second nurse. Dr. Henrickson wrapped a towel around my foot. Amber slid her hands from the gauze to the towel, squeezing so hard the veins on her neck popped out. I should have been scared—but I wasn't. I trusted my team—the people who now held my life in their hands. And whatever the outcome, at any time, I'd know that they did everything they possibly could.

A gasp from the left drew my attention. Kathy stood in the doorway, her expression aghast. She spun on her heels and dashed off, yelling, "I'll call surgery."

Surgery? I thought in dismay. *I hated surgery. They did a lot of cutting in surgery.*

The second nurse was back. She passed a surgical kit off to Dr. H as if it were a baton in a relay race. *I hope you're winning,* I thought.

Dr. Henrickson strode to my right side, and Annie tugged on the foot of the bed so the doctor could move behind me.

"Scott," Dr. H said, "I need to put in a central line."

That's one big-ass needle, I thought.

"There's no time for a numbing agent, so it's going to be painful, but if I don't do it, you'll bleed out before we can get you to surgery," he continued.

My choices are pain or death. So not really a choice at all. Someone lowered the head of my bed until it was below the level of my feet. Dr. Henrickson wiped something down the right side of my neck. Fingers pressed into my neck. They pressed, paused, shifted, and pressed again.

A sharp pinch at the side of my neck. Tears stung my eyes. He had told me it would hurt, but I hadn't understood how much. Pure, unadulterated agony washed over me. Suddenly, it was all real. *This is me,* I thought. *That's my blood on the walls. It's my life they're trying to save.*

As I convulsed from the pain, my vision wavered between a blindingly white light and hypervigilant clarity. Two men raced in with a gurney. I saw them advance on me from the left between spurts of lucidity. I was lifted and shifted. Then we were on the move.

Dr. Henrickson's cool voice: *Stay with us, Scott. Stay with us.*

The flash of lights passed overhead. A chill settled over me.

We rolled out of the elevator into the familiar pallor of the operating room. My teeth chattered around a gaping yawn.

So ... tired, I thought. I shivered violently.

I turned my head a fraction to the left and looked at the surgical nurse standing beside me. My eyelids drooped. I forced them open and searched for her face. She wasn't looking at me. I lifted an arm to draw her attention and watched it quiver in the air. She caught my arm in her hands.

"It's ... c-cold in here," I mumbled through my chattering teeth. She looked at me with wide eyes.

"Stay awake, Scott," she yelled before dashing off. I heard shuffling and rustling from above me and managed to open my eyes wide enough to see a male nurse changing the liter of blood pouring into me.

I felt my eyes droop. I yawned.

The surgical table started moving. I opened my eyes and watched the world tilt around me. Someone inverted the bed so that my head was closest to the ground. I saw fuzzy figures in green scurrying about as my eyelids sagged closed again.

"Hi, Scott," an unfamiliar male voice said, accompanied by a firm hand on my shoulder. I lifted my eyelids one fraction at a time, struggling to focus on the masked face above me. The impression I got was of round jolliness. He had nice, narrow eyes and dark, barely receding hair.

"I'm Dr. Mixter," the voice said. "You don't remember me, but we spent some time together last month." Someone behind him was tinkering with a tray of tools.

A female assistant appeared, the apples of her cheeks peeking out from the top of her mask.

"Everything's okay, Scott," she said, stroking my hair with one hand. "Everything's okay."

Her words reassured me, but her eyes told me otherwise.

A few days later, Dr. Mixter visited me.

"How're you feeling today, Scott?"

"Alive, I guess."

He chuckled, but I hadn't meant it as a joke.

"So, what happened the other day?" I asked as he began gently unwinding the bandage on my left foot. "Why was my foot bleeding?"

"It looked like a staple came loose. Not entirely uncommon, but we sure had to close it right quick." He chuckled. I wondered what part of that statement was meant to be funny.

"Why does the right foot look so different from the left?" I asked. The dissimilarities had bothered me since my first bandage change. While my left foot was cleanly cut through the middle of the arch with a small flap of extra skin used to sew it up, the right was a mutilated stump so short it was hard to tell the difference between the heel and what was now the front end of my foot. The transplanted skin had hair growing from it and looked like someone had taken a meat mallet to it.

"Well, the left didn't have much tissue loss and was a straight, lateral cut and sew," Dr. Mixter said. "There was great debate about whether there should be a BK." He paused, then looked at me with a sideways grin. "Sorry—a below-the-knee amputation. Knowing that you were an athlete, though, I wanted you to have something that you could possibly run on."

He thinks I can run on that? I eyed my mutilated foot.

"It was a bit of a long shot, but I stripped the tissue and padding from the bottom of your foot, then recreated that portion with muscle taken from your abdomen and an eight-by-eight-inch full-thickness skin graft from your thigh. You'll probably have hair growth on the bottom of your foot now, but at least there's something to stand on."

I laughed. It was all I could do. The whole concept was laughable, and yet here was this plastic surgeon who had accomplished it. When faced with the possibility of amputating everything below the knee, my very own mad doctor instead chose to build me a Frankenstein-esque foot from a medley of other body parts.

"There's no guarantee that it will work," Dr. Mixter said when our laughter died down. "You may still lose the lower leg."

I let out the last of my laughter in a deflated huff. The battle still wasn't won. That was the lesson to be taken from the bleeding *incident*, wasn't it? Don't get comfortable—you're not out of the woods yet. It was the mantra of my new life: there are no guarantees. You may still lose.

Yesterday reminded me just how much I didn't want to lose. I wanted to move forward. Were it not for the fast work of the doctors in this hospital, I would have bled out.

As a former high school social studies teacher, I viewed the classroom as my stage, and I challenged my students to become involved with the lectures. On one occasion, while discussing the apartheid government in South Africa and the outspoken and often forgotten founder of the Black Consciousness Movement, Steven Biko, I sat on my chair—which I had placed atop my classroom desk—pressed play on a portable cassette player, and let Peter Gabriel's song *"Biko"* fill the room.

With hands clasped, leaning forward with my elbows on my knees, we listened and then discussed the song. Word of my method reached the executive principal, who called me into her office and asked me to continue being bold in my presentations. That year, the students named me "Best Teacher."

❄

Healing my feet took longer than healing my hands. It took three months after waking from the coma before I was able to try standing for the first time. And I had no concept—not even the slightest inkling—of the excruciating pain I would endure on the vertical table.

The vertical table—*The Torture Table*, as I came to think of it—rested four feet from the floor with a brown leather top that ran nearly seven feet in length. A strap buckled across the middle, and a metal plate stuck up like a footboard at one end. As the table was slowly rotated to the vertical position with me strapped to its surface, I lay still. When I reached a forty-five-degree angle, the weight of my body began to settle into my feet. The closer to vertical I went, the more intensely aware of my mutilated feet I became. At first, it was hyper-awareness, but it quickly translated into a shooting pain that caused both of my calves to seize up.

I grunted as we approached seventy degrees.

"Is something wrong?" Helen asked.

"Mmm..." I moaned through gritted teeth. "God, that hurts."

"It hurts? You might feel some discomfort, but it shouldn't be unbearable."

I didn't want to tell her that unbearable had already come and gone—and we hadn't even reached vertical yet.

"Should I stop?" she asked.

A breath hissed through my clenched teeth. I closed my eyes against the pain. *Should you stop?* I thought. *God, yes, you should fucking stop. Give me another central line, make me lift more weights—literally anything but this.*

I pressed my head back against the leather. "No. Just... keep going."

The table began rotating again. With each degree adjustment, I was forced to bear more weight on my now-healed but still raw feet. I tried not to let the tears seep through my clamped lids. If this was what it took to get back to any semblance of my former life, I would do it—if it didn't kill me first.

Luckily, it didn't. I returned to that table twice a day for the next week. My mind began blockading itself behind brick walls, trying to shield me from the torture. Each time I was taken to the table, a larger and larger part of me was left behind in the room.

I was getting really good at shutting off my brain.

Ten

SCARED SHITLESS

According to Elizabeth Kübler-Ross, the Swiss–American psychiatrist known for her work on near-death studies —which she detailed in her book *On Death and Dying* —there are five stages of grief: denial, anger, bargaining, depression, and acceptance. Not everyone who experiences a life-threatening or life-altering event feels all five stages, and they may occur in a different order than this. For me, denial came fast and hard. This is where I'd find myself stuck for years to come. Even after being forced to confront my amputations head-on, I'd refuse to accept the limitations they imposed.

Work would become my defense mechanism, shielding me from the emotional burden of my new reality. What you refuse to believe can't hurt you—or so I wanted to believe. But unlike the monsters under the bed, this monster didn't disappear when I stopped looking at it. It grew stronger.

From my personal experience, I'd like to add three more stages to the list: fear, guilt, and shame.

I experienced deep-seated fear after learning that my hands and parts of my feet had been amputated. I was afraid of what this change would mean for my future. Afraid of what I had lost.

Afraid of what I had become: the embodiment of many of our worst nightmares.

I experienced guilt when I saw the suffering my family had endured on my behalf. Even when it seemed clear I would live, they continued to be afraid for me because they had no idea how I was going to move forward as a quadruple amputee. Because of me, they had to bear the burden of that worry and fear. And because of me, they still do.

And guilt would haunt me in my relationships beyond my family. It'd resurface every time I saw the impact my illness had on all the people in my life—friends, colleagues, my soccer players. No one was safe from the ramifications of my illness. And with that guilt came shame. Shame becomes murky and can solidify like cement. Shame is what I tried to ignore and hide from others. Shame was what I buried deep within myself as I faked being okay. I was embarrassed to be in a position that forced me to be so different from what I once was.

I saw these three stages firsthand in another, too—a man I met during my stay in the rehab unit of the hospital. His name was Frank, and he was recovering from a massive stroke.

Frank was once a successful businessman. Tired of his hectic life chasing money, he retired and began driving a school bus instead. How he loved his daily route. The raucousness of a bus full of elementary school kids brought him more joy than any sum of money could.

But now, the left side of his body had been left paralyzed. He could no longer speak without slurring, and driving a bus was out of the question.

Each weekday, Frank and I were wheeled to the exercise room and scooted onto a large table. It sat about two feet off the ground and was used mostly for stretching. The top was roughly the size of a California king bed and covered in red pads like those used for tumbling.

The first time we were brought together, Frank was snappish and rude to the physical therapist. I watched him scowl with the right side of his face and saw denial. I also saw loss.

Frank and I warmed up to each other gradually—a slow thawing of stony reserve that turned into lukewarm friendship.

"I hate being an invalid," Frank once confessed to me. "I've lost my confidence."

He shook as he tried to lift and hold his left arm a couple of inches off the table. After ten seconds, he gasped and let his arm fall to the mat. "Am I always going to need someone to dress me and feed me?" he asked.

"Try to avoid that, Frank," I told him. "Bust your ass in here."

"How did you get to the point of managing so well?"

"My goal is to be independent—but to be perfectly honest, I'm scared shitless of what's to come."

Frank ended up leaving the rehab unit before me—because my insurance policy covered a longer stay, I suspect. Frank and I never met again.

After seven days of using *The Torture Table* twice a day, Amy deemed it too easy (where the hell she got that idea is beyond me) and coerced me into trying to walk with her assistance. I had told myself it was all or nothing for the duration of my recovery: *If I don't give it everything I have, there's no point in doing it at all.*

Amy propped her right shoulder under my left arm. With her arm wrapped around my waist, I placed my feet on the ground. As she hauled me up from the sanctuary of my wheelchair and the weight settled into my feet, the pain was instant and unrelenting. After just three excruciating, waddling steps, I was ready to fall to my knees.

Like the pain, though, Amy was unrelenting—and my own pride and determination forced me to meet her step for step. Literally. After a few days of managing to work my way up to walking one lap around the exercise mats, she brought me to the stairwell.

"Up one level and back down," she said as I rested on the landing. "What do you say?"

I stared up the single flight of stairs to the top floor, trying not to count how many steps it would take. I looked down and my eyes fell eight stories to the ground floor below.

All or nothing, man. All or nothing.

I looked up, stared at the first step before me, and said, "I'll walk up to the top. Then I'm walking all the way down to the bottom floor and back up to here."

"Um..." From her cautioning tone, I could tell she was torn between questioning me and empowering me to persevere. But then she spoke definitively: "Let's do it."

With her shoulder for support, I embarked on the second most difficult thing I'd ever done in my life. First was biking the roads around Lake Winnebago. As a cocky undergrad at UW–Oshkosh, I had spouted off (among the wrong crowd) that soccer players were in similar physical condition to professional cyclists. They challenged me to prove it by riding alongside said professional cyclists during a ninety-mile training ride around the lake.

After four hours, I finished the course.

I gained respect from the cyclists for my sport—and an increased respect for cycling. We shook hands after the ride, then went to a bar near campus called Kelly's for a few of their famous Mag Dogs (chili dogs) and frosty mugs of beer.

Unfortunately, now, there was no frothy mug waiting for me at the bottom of the staircase.

As I trudged upward one step at a time, Amy supported me both physically as my crutch and emotionally by remaining quiet and steadfast. As my grunts echoed off the concrete walls around us, I gritted my teeth and trudged on.

This was necessary. This was me versus the disability. For once, I was facing reality—even if it was out of anger.

By the time we reached the ground floor, I realized that the fatigue would potentially prove to be my greatest enemy. The pain was no picnic—it was sheer agony every step of the way. Without the energy to fight through it, though, my hope dwindled. As an athlete and coach, I knew that confidence and a positive attitude tended to separate the strong from the weak.

Failure is not an option, I told myself step after step. *I will not let my disability take this from me. Not now, not ever.*

When my left foot finally hit the landing of the rehab unit on the eighth floor again, followed sluggishly by my right, I nearly collapsed. I was sweating profusely, and I was unequivocally exhausted. My whole body was shaking, my thighs twitching spasmodically, calves trembling with such force it seemed to vibrate up the length of my spine.

"Holy *shit*," Amy spouted.

"You've... got that... right," I injected between exhausted, deep breaths. She helped me fall into the wheelchair and made quick work of getting me back to my room. After helping me crash into bed, she ran off to retrieve a pitcher of ice water.

I ordered and ate two lunches that day—the kitchen made a good grilled cheese. Not chili dogs and beer, but it fit the bill. As did the post-lunch nap.

Eleven

MY OBITUARY

Zenon Wojcik was a lanky man, standing a couple of inches over six feet, with long brown hair streaked with gray that brushed the top of his collar. I first met him a week after what felt like my ascent up Mount Everest, when he strode into my hospital room unannounced.

"Hello there!" he called, moving with an effortless speed that defied logic—like a gust of wind in human form. His long limbs seemed to propel him forward without hurry yet with undeniable purpose. Stopping abruptly at the foot of my bed, he fixed me with a bright-eyed grin.

"Scott?"

"Ye-ah," I answered slowly, trying to orient myself around this unexpected, slightly bizarre man.

"I'm Zenon—Zenon Wojcik from Winkley Prosthetics. And if it's all right with you, I'm going to take you on as a patient."

He beamed. I blinked.

Wojcik from Winkley Prosthetics... take you on as a patient. His words echoed in my sluggish mind. *Patient? Me—a patient for—* Oh. Understanding finally clicked into place. I nodded. At this point, I belonged to so many doctors—what was one more?

"Sure..." I said with raised eyebrows, waiting for him to fill me in on his specialty.

"Great!" he said, already setting up his materials. "Now, I'm here to cast your arms so we can build you a pair of myoelectric hands."

Myoelectric hands. Myos. The myos! A flicker of excitement stirred in my chest. *No more hooks?* I grinned.

"I'm sure you've heard about the myos by now," he continued, glancing at the clunky metal hooks resting on my bedside table. His lip curled in open disdain. "A lot more sophisticated than those things."

I laughed—partly from giddy anticipation, partly from delight at finding a fellow hook-loather. As he worked, he explained the technology, filling in gaps I hadn't even known existed.

Talking with Zenon was like picking the brain of a top soccer coach over a few pints. He was nothing short of brilliant. His passion for his work radiated from him—childlike in its enthusiasm yet tempered by a deep well of knowledge. He never said I couldn't do something. Instead, he saw every challenge as an engineering puzzle waiting to be solved.

By the time he finished casting my arms, I knew one thing: with Zenon as my prosthetist, great things were going to happen.

Almost before I could come down from my Zenon-induced high, he returned the next day—this time bearing an even greater gift.

A device of his own invention.

"This little beauty," he announced, unpacking a meter that resembled an odometer, "will help you get a head start on controlling the myos."

Two wires extended from the meter, each splitting into a total of four small white circles.

"These are receptors," he said, holding up two of them. "Two for each arm. One goes on the muscle group that opens the hand —" he tapped the outside of my forearm, "—and the other on the muscle group that closes it." He tapped the inside. "The meter reads the voltage you generate, which tells the myos how much to open or close."

I held out my arms like an overeager tech geek at Best Buy, itching to play.

Strapped in, I focused on opening my hand—something I hadn't done in ages.

Whoa! The needle on the meter shot to the far right.

I relaxed. It swung back left.

"Cool, huh?" Zenon grinned.

I nodded, transfixed.

"The key," he said, "is finesse. Try moving the needle in small increments. Think about the difference between stroking a cat and pulling a weed—you want that range of control."

I took a deep breath. *Cat. Gentle.* The needle rocketed right.

"That's okay," Zenon reassured me. "Now try bringing it back down... slowly."

I imagined easing my grip. The needle plummeted. Before it hit home, I thought, *Open!*—and it shot back up.

This was going to be harder than I'd expected.

"Good, good," Zenon said, clearly pleased with my fumbles. "It'll take time, but you'll get better. I'll leave this here—let's have the nurses set you up three times a day. Sound good?"

I thought of my already packed rehab schedule, then smiled.

"Sounds excellent."

"Super!" He spun toward the door. "Practice, practice, practice. Enjoy!"

Enjoy I did. The more I played with Zenon's device, the more it reminded me of controlling a soccer ball—the precision, the feel, the muscle memory. The finesse needed to master the meter was like bending a free kick around a wall of defenders. I loved it.

Distractions became my morphine. And this one—right under soccer-related activities—was exactly the dose I needed.

"Wonder!"

I flinched in surprise at the sound of my old nickname being hollered from the door. I'd earned the moniker as a high schooler after hitting a bicycle kick for a goal in my senior gym class (horizontal, with my back parallel to the ground). Living in a state where baseball, basketball, and football were the main sports of merit at the time, my classmates' only familiarity with soccer was through their phys-ed classes. Naturally, my acrobatics startled them. Hence, I was tabbed "Wonder Boy," which was soon shortened simply to "Wonder."

I looked up to see a burly man with reddish hair steering a wheelchair chaotically through the door. My jaw dropped. *Jim?*

It couldn't be. Jim Porter and I had played together before college. He was a moving Rock of Gibraltar—few made it past him as our center back, and many left the field black and blue.

Before I could get a word out, three more came careening through the door: Barry Gruetzmacher, a long spaghetti-noodle of a man; Rainer Gola, the strongman from Germany and our steadfast goalkeeper; and Jeff Dix, another of our staunch back line. I was dumbfounded. These guys lived at least three hours away. How—and why—the hell were they *here?*

My mother had told me that when I was in the coma, a bunch of my old teammates had come to visit, thinking it would be the last time they'd see me. But now I was awake—and they didn't need to fear for my life.

"Get your lazy ass outta bed, man!" Rainer said in his German accent, still thick after decades in the States. "We're going out!"

I was so surprised I could barely get a grip on what was happening. "Where'd you get that wheelchair?" I asked.

Jim shrugged with a smirk. "Eh, we made a deal with the head lady out there." He gestured over his shoulder to the hallway outside.

"I promised her I'd keep you in the chair. Got it?"

I just laughed. With how much pain walking caused me, I didn't anticipate wanting to deviate from that plan.

"So, where should we go?" Jeff asked.

Finally, something I had an answer to. "The Camaraderie. I've been *jonesing* for some handmade fried cheese curds."

On the way out, the head nurse for the night called out, "Hey! Remember our deal, all right?"

"We promise he'll stay in the chair," Jim replied. "But we can't guarantee in what condition he'll return," he added with a smirk.

It had been months since my last alcoholic drink. One Captain Morgan and Coke in, and I was sliding effortlessly past tipsy and into drunk. I may have broken a glass accidentally—a casualty of my unfamiliarity with the myoelectric hands I was now outfitted with—amid all the ruckus we caused, but I did stay put in my wheelchair.

Being out of the hospital was intoxicating in itself. Coupled with the company of old friends (of both the human and libation variety), all my concerns evaporated. It didn't matter if I was the only guy in a wheelchair or that I didn't have hands. Surrounded by my soccer family, I was the same old Wonder I'd always been.

We reminisced. We discussed our continued frustration with the U.S. Men's National Soccer Team and our applause for the Women's Team. As if we'd never missed a beat, we sat and bull-shitted about everything—everything except my disability, that is. I didn't know if they were being polite or reading my attitude, but ignoring my current state was as refreshing as the cool drink I couldn't feel in my prosthetic hand.

As promised, I returned belted into the wheelchair and a bit toasted from the outing. After the guys said their goodbyes, I leaned back in my bed and reveled in the long-forgotten sensation of being truly relaxed. It felt so good to be carefree for a few hours. I thought about going back to my old life in my new condition and felt only eager anticipation. With the taste of rum still on my tongue, I felt kind of invincible.

I looked to the door and considered the world beyond it. *You know what?* I thought. *Why the hell not.*

Having been in bed only a few minutes, I threw the covers off my legs and slid my feet to the floor once again. I pushed myself up from the bed until I was standing. I bobbled slightly—both from my unfamiliarity with standing and my alcohol intake—and gripped the bedrail for balance. I was up. I was standing on my own two feet. I don't know if it was the Captain Morgan and Cokes numbing me, but it didn't even hurt.

Grinning dopily, I started to shuffle toward the door. *I'm gonna give the nurses one hell of a show.*

Before passing through the doorway, my eyes landed on the faux-fur bunny slippers my little sister, Lisa, had sent me a few days earlier. They were a few sizes smaller than my normal ten— chosen in an attempt to fit my newly stunted limbs. I shoved them on and continued to the hallway.

As I reached the nurses' station, I found a couple of familiar faces bent over charts.

I lifted my nose and semi-slurred, "Hello, ladies. What's up?"

Their eyeballs bulged. Carolyn did a double take, shaking her head and blinking to make sure I was really there. "Looks like *you* are," she replied. "All six feet of you."

Cheryl rushed around the desk to help me. I backed away from the counter before she could reach me, declining her help.

"Well, look at you," Cheryl said, impressed by my stability.

"Yup." I turned on my feet and danced my way down the hall à la Kevin Bacon in *Footloose*. Cheryl stayed close, ready to rescue me if I started to fall. I made it all the way back to my bed without so much as a bobble. Cheryl helped me kick off my slippers and slide under the covers.

"This came today," she said, handing me an envelope with my mother's handwriting on it.

I used my teeth to open the envelope, and a newspaper clipping fell out. It was from the *Oshkosh Northwestern,* my alma mater's daily newspaper. The article, written by the editor, Jim Metz, was titled *"As an undergraduate, he made a mark on Oshkosh."* I unfolded it and began to read:

Seldom does a person come to UW–Oshkosh as an undergraduate and put a permanent mark on the lives of hundreds of Oshkosh people before graduating. Scott Martin did. I am one he touched.

When classmates got to know Oshkosh nightlife, Scott got involved with the then-fledgling Oshkosh Youth Soccer Club. In his first year, 1980, he coached two teams—one comprising eight- and nine-year-olds, the other ten- and eleven-year-olds. The next year, he was elected to the board of directors, and it was here I met him.

He did not introduce me to soccer but immersed me in it. He not only coached, but he also officiated. I joined him in the task of recruiting, training, and scheduling the referees. It may have seemed unusual—a young college athlete allied with this paunchy middle-ager—but we put a great deal of effort into our duties.

In 1983, Scott was elected president of the club, presiding over an ever-enlarging program. And when it was difficult to find enough coaches, he took on even more responsibility. One season, he coached four teams. That's about seventy youngsters under the supervision of this undergraduate who went to practices and games all around the city on a bike.

His dedication was total, his example inspiring.

Scott Martin is now mending. He's being fitted with artificial arms. He's undergoing intensive therapy, both occupational and physical. And he's active in coaching his team. Even from his hospital bed, their playing and their success are not just on

Martin's mind—they're receiving his instruction, his insight, his special inspiration.

I sucked in a ragged breath and let the article fall to my lap. *This could have been my obituary.* I shook my head to dislodge the morose thought. It had been some night—a little taste of freedom and a big reminder of what I was capable of achieving.

UW–Oshkosh was where I grew up. During the three years after high school when my focus was solely on playing soccer, I worked at night to pay the bills so I could be on the field during the day. I was the disc jockey at a fledgling disco called Gritz's, owned and managed by my teammate Barry Gruetzmacher's family. Even though we were only teenagers, we had hopes of making it the hottest place in the region.

It was the night before Gritz's grand opening, and we were doing a dry run to be sure all the kinks were worked out before the following evening. With the twelve-inch extended version of Donna Summer's "Love to Love You Baby" flowing from the white speakers that mimicked the Death Star from *Star Wars*, hung above the corners of the dance floor, I reentered the bar after hitting the bathroom. Turning left toward the booth to check the record as it spun on the turntable, something else caught my attention—or rather, someone.

Like a 1950s Audie Murphy movie, I fell in love at first sight with a high school senior with dark, wavy hair, sporting a white T-shirt, denim jacket, and worn blue jeans—paired with a smile that lit up her eyes.

Her name was Sue, and she lived in the quaint village of Junction City, twenty miles north of the dance club in Wisconsin Rapids. After our first meeting, we ran into each other occasionally. We only went out on one official date, but we knew each other as if we had grown up together. Whenever our paths crossed, we talked for hours and danced all night long. I thought I was too immature for her—and I was right. I didn't want it to go badly, so I let life happen. Days and months gave way to years, decades.

Even after I left for Oshkosh, I thought about her for years to come. She would forever remain tucked away in a special place in my heart. I believed we were soulmates, me and Sue from JC. *I wonder if she felt the same.*

Two days after my drunken escapade, I was summoned by the rehab department head for a "chat." As I toddled into the conference room, I tried not to feel like a schoolboy about to get his backside whacked by a paddle. I was certain that the focus of the meeting would be my night out and less-than-sober return. In truth, I didn't really know what was allowed and what wasn't.

Greeted by the smiling faces of my rehab staff—and the not-so-smiling department head—I did my best to bite back the excuses ready to explode from within me. I wasn't really sorry, but I knew I would be if I got on these people's bad side.

"Welcome, Scott," the department head said. "Have a seat."

When I was done situating myself in the interrogation chair, he added, "You look like you're getting around pretty well these days."

"You bet," I replied with a sheepish smile. After breaking through my fear barrier with the help of Captain Morgan, walking had turned into a mere feat of endurance. The goal had become to walk farther and longer each day.

"Carolyn has told me about your recent night of... debauchery." He chose his words carefully. I tried to affect an expression of humility. "After having spoken with everyone here, I think I speak for us all when I say it's about time we kick you out."

I froze. *Kick me out?* Had my "debauchery" really been that big of a deal? Enough to warrant expulsion?

As I looked from one medical professional to the next, I saw that a smile was creeping up on everyone's face. The realization slowly dawned on me.

"Are you saying... I'm ready to be *discharged?*"

"You bet," the department head said with a chuckle, clearly mocking my earlier response.

I laughed—threw my head back and let out a whooping cry of joy. *I'm a fucking graduate. I passed!*

And my reward would be the greatest of all: reclaiming my life.

Twelve

THE FOG ROLLS IN

I held two positions at the university: assistant hall director and head soccer coach. It was a constant juggle, but I had managed it well. Even though it now took me more than an hour to dress myself, I was deft at the art of time management. While I was away, a variety of colleagues from the housing department—Tom and Sue Peck and their three boys—plus multiple soccer players, fed my cats and cleaned their litter box.

Upon my return to my dorm apartment, I was greeted by the sweet purrs of my four-legged pals, asking me where the hell I'd been for the last five months. The first thing I did was turn on the stereo, slide on my headphones, and listen to *Dark Side of the Moon* by Pink Floyd while stretched out on the sofa—ensuring my escape from any inquisitive phone calls or knocks at my door for the next while.

After returning to work, I had to put in longer hours—which I didn't mind. It was far easier to devote myself to my work than to ruminate over the happenings of the last several months. I gave myself virtually no time for grief, anxiety, or insecurity—even when everyone in public was staring at my hands. My work forced me to create a daily routine, which became my saving grace. I began to follow this regimen robotically, fully using work as a means of avoidance. I was teetering on the edge of complete burnout, just about ready to topple over at any minute at the brush of a feather.

Turns out that feather would come sooner than I thought. Walking down the hall at 6:45 a.m., I was too absorbed in planning my day to react fast enough to the two girls who came sashaying around the corner ahead of me. And they, in turn, were too caught up in their conversation to notice me.

All I caught was a glimpse of blonde hair in my path. I stumbled to my right in an effort to avoid a collision, but I reacted too slowly. Our shoulders jostled, and I staggered sideways, barely able to catch my balance.

The girl I had bumped gasped and lifted a pink-manicured hand toward her friend for balance.

"Excuse me," I mumbled as I righted myself and continued past them.

As we continued on our separate ways, I heard a voice cry from behind me. "Ewww!"

I started to turn, curious what had caused her disgust.

"That man with no hands *touched* me!"

Her words reverberated toward me—*through* me. Her words *were* me. She was disgusted by *me*.

Shrinking into myself, I put my head down and pulled the myoelectric hands toward my stomach. A cold sweat broke out across my forehead.

I felt my heart race and dove for the sanctity of my hall director's office. I fumbled with the keys—*Damn fucking robotic hands.* It took too many tries and too much concentration to single out the correct one. The usual sound of the opening and closing of the myos now echoed through the hallway like the screech of a cat.

I pinched the key between two fingers and a thumb. I fought

to navigate it into the keyhole and turn the lock. I imagined the eyes of the entire student body on me—staring at my mannequin-like hands, judging me for my incompetence and disability. I felt inept and isolated. I was an outsider. I was the campus freak.

The key finally slid in. I turned the latch. I rammed my shoulder into the door with unnecessary force and stumbled across the threshold. I hastily pushed the door shut behind me. I wanted to lock the world out.

My arms shook as I set my key ring on the desk and collapsed into a chair. The only sounds were my panting and the creak of my hands as they spasmed uncontrollably because I was so frazzled. In a string of eight words, that girl had sliced right through the sheltering façade I'd hidden behind. All that false bravado and purported self-confidence vanished in the blink of an eye. Hearing her words forced me to glimpse the very thing I'd been avoiding: my shattered self-image and the deep, dark depression slowly rising within me.

I'm a quadruple amputee, I thought. *I'm severely disabled.*

My brain shut down. I stared ahead, sitting in the dark office. The phone rang more than a dozen times. I didn't answer. I had no idea how long it had been before I rose from the chair to turn on the light.

Maybe I needed this kick in the balls. I was faking everything —everything I'd felt, everything I pretended to be. I had been doing a great imitation of myself while constantly flashing an empty smile. I failed to analyze, adjust, or rebuild. And I continued to bury myself in work rather than deal with the beginning of a deep, dark depression.

A few weeks later, I'd convinced myself that my constant feeling of being in a hazy fog was normal. It was like living with cotton balls stuffed in my ears and dark goggles on: everything was muffled and unclear. I felt like I was walking underwater.

The Fog, as I began to call it, rolled in each morning when I donned my prosthetics. I could do everything seamlessly now, without thought. I trained myself to use the myos just as I had once learned to manipulate a soccer ball—I no longer needed my brain. Every time I looked down at them, I checked out, still refusing to accept that part of my life.

I had never been able to fully shake what the plastic surgeon had said about my right foot: *You might still lose your entire lower leg.* It haunted me. Every morning, I made a point of examining the foot before dressing. The primary concern was blood flow through the extremity. I examined the bottom briefly, then watched the artery located just under the skin at the upper heel pump blood into what remained of my foot. It was always a moment of dispelling relief to see it gently throbbing beneath the skin—a sign that I was going to keep my foot another day.

This morning, though, something was different. On the base of my foot where the arch used to be, about the size of a dime, was a deep red hole. Leaning closer, I could see the muscle tissue that had once been part of my abdomen stretching beneath the skin that used to belong to my right thigh.

How did a hole like that develop and I didn't even feel it? I thought. *Something so severe should have caused me pain, no?*

And yet I felt nothing. I knew the poor design of the prosthetic inserts caused my foot to pivot when I walked, but I always wore socks. Shouldn't that have prevented this?

I grabbed the phone next to my bed and called my doctor. Two days later, I was led into an exam room to be... examined. Obviously.

Everything about that visit is a blur. I sat soaking in *The Fog* as he examined my foot, cleaning and debriding the wound. He diagnosed the hole as an "ulceration." He prescribed antibiotics to keep an infection at bay. A nurse would drop by my apartment each day to change the dressing, he said. *Great—one more thing to avoid thinking about.* I tightened the leash on my emotions and carried on.

Tom Peck was the director of Murray Hall. He was also nearly seven feet tall and still holds the rebound record at UW–Eau Claire from his college basketball days. Tom, his wife Sue, and their sons Matthew, Spencer, and Jeremiah had become family to me before any of this happened. I coached Matt's U16 soccer team and very gratefully attended the occasional home-cooked dinner.

Succumbing to the fate of my new hands, I lost my driver's license and needed to rely on others to get around.

After wandering through a nearby Target with me, Tom drove us to a large, empty parking lot on campus and got out of the car.

"Let's see what you can do," he beckoned from his open driver's door. "Move your ass behind the wheel."

"Hell yes! Let's do this," I said, a huge smile spreading across my face.

Chuckling like a madman, I slid across the front bench seat and into the driver's side of his navy-blue family station wagon.

Driving straight forward was easy, but trying to turn the wheel in my usual hand-over-hand fashion was a disaster. Once I had gripped the wheel, I couldn't open my hands quickly enough to adjust their position and continue the turn. The result was me helplessly twisted in a car that was quickly careening off its designated course.

This led to our discovering that I had also lost my touch on the brake pedal when I stomped down far too hard to keep the car from running into a light post.

Tom and I flopped in our seats like rag dolls, looked at each other with wide, bulging eyes, and promptly burst into raucous laughter.

"Oops," I said sheepishly. "Sorry about that."

While I made attempt after unsuccessful attempt at turning the car, Tom continued to laugh so hard that tears began pouring down his cheeks. As I watched his head bobble back and forth like he belonged on the dash, I felt minor concern that he was in danger of a concussion.

"Okay, Mr. Race Car," he said after my umpteenth attempt. "We need to smooth out your technique."

"What I need is a spinner knob like they have on ski boats— something that lets me turn faster. Only we replace the knob with a U-shaped handle that has a grip on one side so I can grab it and use it to turn the wheel without needing to let go."

Like magic, Zenon—the prosthetist who had fitted me with the myoelectric hands—had my exact proposed design ready the following week. Tom and I rigged it to his steering wheel and continued to practice.

Two weeks later, Sue took me to my driving test. Upon greeting me, the proctor's only comment was, "I can't say that I've tested anyone with your type of disability, Mr. Martin."

I shrugged and distracted him with the contraption on the steering wheel.

He didn't say a word for the entire duration of the test, only taking his eyes off the road once to jot a few notes on his clipboard after I successfully parallel parked on our return.

"Well, Scott," he said, "I see no problem with having you behind the wheel."

Thirteen

THE HOLE DEEPENS

"Hey, Bonzo!" a man's voice hollered into the phone when I picked up.

"Savrsnik?" I asked, thinking of the only one who would call me Bonzo for no apparent reason. "Holy *shit!*"

"Yeah, man—" he said. "I'm gonna be in Eau Claire for a meeting next week. Are you free for lunch on Monday?"

The last time I had visited Scott and his wife, Jill, was before I moved to Eau Claire—long before my illness. I wasn't sure if he knew what had happened to me, but I decided not to ask.

"Sounds good," I responded, not giving him the details.

I knew I should have asked.

At noon on Monday, I was roused by a booming knock at my apartment door. Using the inside portion of the myo with my hand closed—my solution for turning a round doorknob with no wrist—I opened the door to the grinning, mustached face of my former college roommate. We hugged and patted each other on the back. As we separated, I could feel the hesitation in my usually jocular friend. Scott's eyes locked onto the myos.

The seconds ticked by as we stood in awkward silence.

I closed my eyes briefly, steeling myself for the conversation that was about to come, and said, "Come on into my humble abode."

Scott seemed to shudder back to life at my words. While the silence had been broken, the dividing cruelty of its cause-and-effect remained strong—driving a cold fissure between old friends.

"Have a seat," I said, gesturing to the sofa and watching as he lowered himself onto the cushions, his face frozen in an expression of horror and shock. I looked into his eyes, flicking between the myos and my face.

"You didn't know... did you?"

He looked up at me with distraught, pained eyes. "Is this a joke?"

I winced. *Wouldn't that be great?* I thought. *If all of this were just some elaborate joke?*

After taking a seat in the chair across from the sofa, I took a deep breath and told him the greatly abbreviated story of the past several months of my life. As I spoke, Scott shook his head back and forth, eyes downcast and brow furrowed, trying to absorb what I was telling him.

When my recount came to an end, he simply sat quietly until time seemed to dull the sting of my words.

"No." He shook his head vehemently. "No. No, no, *no!*"

I looked down at the myos as the rift between us deepened.

After another painfully protracted pause, he murmured, "How did you... contract the bacteria?"

I looked at him with a sad understanding. Sitting with Scott, sharing my story and watching it tear at him, I could again see the ripple effect of my illness. With each passing day, the reverberations spread further and further—and the distance between me and the people they touched grew wider and wider.

I wanted to apologize for the pain I was causing him. I felt terrible—but I didn't want to make a habit of apologizing for my illness. So instead, I apologized for something else.

"It's complicated, buddy. I'm afraid I can't go out to lunch. A meeting came up this morning. Sorry to bail on you, man."

There was no meeting, and I'm sure he knew that. But I could tell he was uncomfortable seeing me like this and needed time to process what he had just learned. I understood that—and I wanted him to know I did.

He studied me for a moment, then nodded slowly. "Yeah, sure. It's no problem."

Together we stood from our seats. I showed him to the door and watched as he walked slowly down the hall toward the exit.

After muscling through the first few months of my new life, I began to feel invigorated—mostly because of work and the current soccer season. It seemed as though *The Fog* had passed, and suddenly I felt ready to take on anything.

When the hole on my right foot resurfaced, I refused to let it intrude on my renewed positivity. I bought my own tape and four-by-four gauze pads to cover the wound as the nurse had done each day and continued as if nothing was wrong. I kept it clean and convinced myself it wasn't getting wider, deeper, redder. It was the start of the season, and we were kicking ass.

There's no way I'm about to let up now, I thought.

As deep as the hole in my foot was growing, I threw myself even deeper into my work. And the program thrived because of it. While I was hospitalized, our goalkeeper Diane Kelsch had been named All-American, and my assistant, Cindy Koperski, while filling in for me, was tabbed Conference Coach of the Year. The program was still on track.

In preparation for a difficult schedule, we fared well in preseason matches against a team from Russia that included players from their National Team and the University of Minnesota—a Division I school. As young as many of my players were (seventeen of the twenty-two on the final roster were freshmen and sophomores), we started the season with flying colors, winning seven of our first eight matches.

After returning from a successful trip to St. Louis, I opened the regular Tuesday national ranking email and scanned for our name on the list. We'd started the season ranked nineteenth in the country. As my eyes crept down the list, I nodded at the top three teams, scoffed at the fourth, and grumbled at the fifth and sixth.

Then I saw the seventh: *UW–Eau Claire.*

"Boom!" I shouted to the empty soccer office. I nearly jumped up to dance around on my half-feet—only the thought that someone might walk past the door kept me in my seat. We were seventh in the nation. Up twelve spots since the start of the season.

"Hot *damn!*"

This was the third year of the program. Things were still on track, even after everything that had happened. It was all the vindication I needed to continue diving headlong into my work. Disabled or not, we'd broken the top ten. Next stop? National champions.

Unfortunately, my foot had other ideas. Shortly after receiving the news of our ranking, the rancid smell of infection took hold. It was as if my foot were finally begging for attention to its critical state—and critical it was.

Dr. Joseph Rucker appeared to be about ten years older than me, with narrow blue eyes and a round, balding head. The way his staff spoke his name with such reverence made it clear he was well respected in the local medical community—and likely beyond.

"This is quite impressive," he said, examining the patchwork foot—compliments of Dr. Mixter. "Something you really have to see to believe, I'd say. But let's have a look at the troublemaker."

I leaned back on my elbows for support as he unearthed the hole, hoping desperately that what he had to say wouldn't be life-altering. My life had been altered quite enough for one year—for a lifetime, actually.

"Ah—here we go."

After a moment, he sat up and gently lowered my leg onto the table. I felt as if I were crawling, click by click, to the top of a roller coaster, gearing up for an organ-sloshing fall.

"That's definitely an infection, as you said," he began. *Click.*

"It's quite deep." *Click, click.*

"You've had damage to both the skin and the underlying muscle tissue. It looks like it'll require surgery to correct."

Whoosh. Down I plummeted. *I didn't fucking sign up for this,* I thought.

But I *had* signed up for it. I'd kept walking on the foot. I'd known exactly how bad that hole was, and I was too busy finally feeling good—finally emerging from *The Fog*—to do anything about it.

With this news, *The Fog* heard its calling. I could feel it pushing its way up against the door of the room, desperate to get close and envelop me once again.

I couldn't bear the thought of surgery now—not in the middle of the season, and especially not when we were doing so well.

"Scott." Dr. Rucker called me out of my head. I looked at him and sighed.

"You will need surgery."

He seemed to be studying me—examining whatever was showing on my face. I nodded and cleared my throat.

"But—" he continued before I could speak, "it can be postponed for a short period of time. If you'd prefer, we could put you on antibiotics and keep a close eye on it until the timing gets better."

I stared at him, eyes lighting up, wondering what reason he thought I had for ducking out of surgery. I didn't even care—all I needed to hear was that there was an alternative.

"I want you to know I don't recommend this option. The longer we wait to perform surgery, the greater the risk of complications later on."

Complications. I had a pretty good sense of just how bad "complications" could be. *Am I willing to risk losing my entire lower leg for the chance to finish the season?* I had already lost so much.

There was a chance I'd lose my leg if I postponed the surgery, but I was almost guaranteed to miss the rest of the season if I elected to have it now. Neither option left me with a clear choice, and I was going to be wrong either way.

I left with a prescription for potent antibiotics and instructions to call if any changes occurred. I was taking a gamble—one that could cost me my leg—but soccer was the one thing keeping me afloat. I wasn't sure I could stand to lose it. Not yet.

I was handling it all fine. The long hours at work, the pressures of the season, the never-ending problem-solving my disability required.

So why was I lying on the floor having a panic attack?

It was my lunch break. I'd just finished eating and settled in to watch a few more minutes of CNN. Nothing out of the ordinary had happened over the last several days—no new trauma, no side effects from the antibiotics Dr. Rucker had prescribed. The season was still going well, the team performing above expectations. We were on track to be invited to the National Tournament at the end of the season.

Then my heart stopped.

Like someone had flipped a switch. On one second, off the next.

Then off again for two seconds.

Panicking, breath held, I waited to feel it start up again. A few moments later, it resumed beating—this time much faster than before. Terror rushed through me.

I'd been told my pulse had stayed at one hundred and seventy beats per minute for an entire week while I was in the coma. Such strain had to have taken days—years—off my life already. What would be the consequence of it happening again now?

I tried to breathe slowly, to think calm thoughts. *It's probably nothing to worry about, right?*

Nowadays, everything felt like something to worry about.

It's stress, the voice in my head said. *You're doing too much, not giving yourself time to relax.*

Relaxing wasn't in my schedule for a reason. When you relax, you give yourself time to think. I needed to function, not think.

I pushed myself upright, standing on wobbly legs. Everything around me was slightly fuzzy. I shut off the television and slowly made my way to the soccer office.

The voice in my head started again: *You should see a doctor, you fool. Hearts aren't supposed to do that. Don't ignore this, or else...*

But I couldn't let the disability beat me. *You're being stupid.*

I ignored the badgering and unlocked the office door. I had to keep moving forward.

With only five matches left in the season, I couldn't afford to slow down now.

The first match after my heart-palpitation scare was at Marquette, another Division I school. I'd scheduled the game to prepare us for the homestretch—it would set us up to be one of the only sixteen colleges invited to the National Tournament at the time. Perhaps I'd been wrong to schedule such a challenging opponent, especially on the road—and on artificial turf instead of grass. But our team was strong, and training was as good as ever. We had to see how far we could go; otherwise, what was the point?

The match ended in a blink. Marquette scored five goals. We scored zero.

Eight days later, we had another away match, this time against a top-ten Division III university—Gustavus Adolphus. We managed to score a goal, but one wasn't enough to compensate for the four they put on us. It was devastating. A big blow to the team's confidence. On the tail of twelve wins, two ties, and three losses, we'd just lost two matches in a row. With only three remaining in the season, we were in trouble.

I patted slouched backs and rounded shoulders as we loaded onto the coach bus after the Adolphus game.

"It's alright," I kept saying. "Two losses don't mean it's over. Keep your heads up."

A few players met my eyes with weak smiles. Some tried to carry the torch of optimism. But we all knew *over* was exactly what it was.

I was shattered. Deflated. Exhausted. As I glanced around at their sullen faces, I saw my own attitude reflected back at me.

I did this, I thought, turning to stare out the window of the bus. *Me. I'm responsible for their defeat. I should have scheduled weaker opponents to pad our record. I set the goal and failed to guide us to it.*

A few days later, we managed to rally, pulling off a 9–1 win against UW–Platteville, immediately followed by a 2–0 win against UW–River Falls the next day. Both were Division III teams, though, and neither win would be enough to salvage our season.

After unbandaging my right foot the night of the River Falls match, I discovered that the infection had returned. The stench was back. The hole had also deepened so that now, when I peered into it, I could see bone showing through the dark red meat of the muscle.

"*Shit,*" I muttered under my breath.

I dropped my face into my hands, then recoiled—shocked for a moment by the cold rubber of the myos. Everything felt constricted. It felt as if all the pressure I had been denying for so long was suddenly piled on top of my skull. I sighed and slowly made my way to my pillow.

The Fog had returned, and I felt myself sinking deeper into it.

Two days after our season came to a close, with no invitation to the National Tournament, I returned to Dr. Rucker's office. This time, when he proposed surgery, I didn't argue.

Fourteen

ON MY KNEES

Fred Rogers, of *Mr. Rogers' Neighborhood*, once said, "Part of the problem with the word *'disabilities'* is that it immediately suggests an inability to see or hear or walk or do other things that many of us take for granted. But what of people who can't feel? Or talk about their feelings? Or manage their feelings in constructive ways? What of people who aren't able to form close and strong relationships? And people who cannot find fulfillment in their lives, or those who have lost hope, who live in disappointment and bitterness and find in life no joy, no love? These, it seems to me, are the real disabilities."

My question: Where does this leave people whose physical disabilities become their emotional disabilities?

Like rescuers to a man who's fallen overboard, people began to flock to my side after surgery on my "bad" foot. My apartment was too small for a wheelchair to make sense, and using crutches was out because of the excessive pressure applied to my hands, so I was forced to get around on my knees. Colleagues brought me groceries and, on occasion, did my cooking and dishes. I sensed my family taking stock of me whenever we spoke on the phone or got together. Everyone hovered—uncertain, waiting for a sign.

They did have cause for concern—more so than I realized at the time. My team noticed, though, and our season hurt for it.

At the start of my third season back, I was forced to face my amputations more than ever. Soccer had been my one haven on campus, my refuge from strangers' perceived peeping eyes. Now it was unfamiliar territory.

I found myself standing before a group of young women I hadn't known before the illness. They stared back at me blankly. I mean, what would any player think of a quadruple amputee for a coach? I saw myself as I imagined they saw me: amputee first, soccer coach second.

Because I failed to recruit a top goal scorer and didn't recognize the lingering effects of a foot injury to our top returning forward, we had issues heading into the season. Others could score, but moving one or two players forward lessened the quality of the midfield.

And thus, as I slid beneath *The Fog,* we slid down the rankings. We ended the season with a measly ten wins—the poorest showing of the program thus far. As we gathered to say our brief goodbyes at the season's end, I gazed, eyes unfocused, at the players sitting around me. Through my own obscurity, everything seemed as it should be. In a life void of emotions, it's easy to overlook those of others.

Life returned to campus after winter break just as it had left: in a trickle followed by a flood. I opened the soccer office door and set about the routine tasks of each day. After going through the mail and finding nothing of interest, I turned to the school newspaper for a momentary indulgence. *The Spectator* was student-run and, naturally, student-focused. After skimming the front page, I flipped to the sports section.

And there it was—front page, above the fold—an article that would change my life.

In it, two of our players were quoted as saying they'd lost interest in the program. Among them was one of our team captains. Her main contributing quote read, "The focus is too much on winning. We just want to have fun."

I read those two sentences over and over again. *The focus is too much on winning. We just want to have fun.* It was a slap in the face—to the university, to the student-athletes and the athletic department, to her teammates and the coaching staff. Athletics was funded by the school and the student body; they weren't paying for the players to "just have fun." Representing UW–Eau Claire in a varsity sport was an honor. I was blown away by the arrogance and audacity of such a statement. I was also disappointed that these students had conveniently forgotten the list of priorities I had indoctrinated them with during recruiting:

Family
Studies
Soccer
Social Life

I didn't understand. I didn't understand any of it.

A shadow from the doorway drew my attention. A tall, slender woman with bobbed, silvering hair stepped into the office. By the sympathetic expression on her face, she knew about the article.

"May I sit?" she asked, settling herself on the edge of the blue sofa. She took a moment to collect her thoughts. Marilyn was my boss and the type of person who always spoke with conviction and forethought—qualities I greatly admired in her.

After a lengthy pause, she told me of a similar situation that had happened to her in her coaching days. A student reporter had published comments from her players that negatively slanted the story while failing to ask Marilyn for her own comment before printing the piece.

"Deal with it in the manner that you feel is right," she advised me, "but don't do it through the press." Her expression was solemn and stern. I wasn't sure if it was a boss's order or a colleague's concerned advice she was offering. Either way, I nodded my agreement. She stood and left me to my convictions.

The columnist who had written the story called me the next morning, fishing for a response. I listened to the faceless voice and tried not to think of him as a scapegoat for my frustrations.

When he paused for my response, I spoke through gritted teeth. "Don't you think it would have been responsible journalism to have asked my opinion before you went to press? Unless, of course, you were more interested in reporting only one side of the story."

I let the implication linger just long enough to prove he had no ready reply, then added, "As to your question—no comment."

No follow-up story was run.

I called the players who had appeared in the article. Both answering machines dumped me to voicemail. I left them each a message, calmly asking for them to return my call. If they had issues with the team or my coaching style, they needed to bring those concerns to me. I hoped that after an open conversation we could resolve the problems and move forward.

Neither of them returned my calls.

The following morning, I submitted my resignation to Marilyn.

I was past running on fumes. I was empty. I needed a change.

The following week, I returned to the soccer office one last time to pack my things. Coincidentally, I was leaving at the time I'd always intended to go. Different terms, but still my timeline, I supposed. Build a strong program, then move up the ladder in three to five years. I could still remember the fearless, determined head coach who had set those goals. If only he'd had an idea of where life would actually lead him.

I smiled. He'd never have let it stop him.

With two boxes on the cart at my feet, I shut the soccer office door, firmly placing the University of Wisconsin–Eau Claire behind me.

I left with no regrets, but over time, one would grow: to this day, I still wish I had written to the graduated players, thanking them for their dedication and support in helping me transition back from the hospital.

I wasn't sad when I returned to my off-campus apartment. I wasn't angry or even disappointed. I felt nothing. Looking back, the newspaper article truly wasn't what led me to resign—and it certainly wasn't the onset of my depression. It was just another interlocking Lego block in the whole ordeal.

Over the next few weeks, I applied for half a dozen college coaching positions and attended three interviews. I knew nothing would come from them after overhearing one athletic director say to his secretary following my interview, "Why did you have me speak with a guy with no hands?"

When the phone rang a few days after returning from my interviews, I dreaded another check-up call. My resignation from UW–Eau Claire only made those already concerned for my well-being even more anxious. I was too tired to explain how little it mattered to yet another worried loved one.

My mother's voice held none of the exaggeratedly upbeat tones people had begun to adopt around me. She sounded as deflated as I felt.

"Mom?" I asked, all thoughts of my well-being dispelled by concern for hers. "What's wrong?"

"Don…" she petered off, her voice thick and hoarse.

She paused.

I waited, listening to her ragged breathing.

"Don has cancer. It's well progressed. You need to come home."

I found Don seated in the living room chair at his and my mother's home in Janesville. His only recognizable feature was his usual plaid button-up shirt and suspendered slacks; the rest of what slumped before me was a defeated semblance of the man I'd known for the past decade.

I pulled a wooden chair from the dining room and sat facing him. He peered up at me with gaunt, dejected eyes.

"Hi, Scotty. How are you?"

"I'm fine, Don. I see the chemo isn't fun." I gestured to the red puke pail by his feet.

"Not fun at all. Your mother had to clean up my mess right over there when I couldn't hold my bowels. She has to help me too much."

I could empathize. I had no intention of offering the fake optimism that typically followed—no rah-rah speech, no false bravado. Don deserved better. He deserved honesty.

"Don, I came to tell you how much respect I have for you. Not many people can handle my mother."

He chuckled, a phlegmy sound that resonated from deep in his lungs.

"After I woke up from the coma, you came to the hospital and shaved my face every day," I told him. I needed him to know that what he'd done for me, both in the hospital and out, was invaluable.

"Well, you couldn't do it yourself," he replied. "And you needed to keep your looks up for all the good-looking nurses you had."

I smiled and felt the sting of tears welling up. "That I did, that I did." I paused. "I respect you, Don. And I love you. You're a good man."

I stood from my chair, feeling both lighter and weaker for

having said those things—lighter for knowing that now he knew exactly how I felt; weaker for the farewell shadowing our conversation.

I placed my right hand delicately on his thinned shoulder. I leaned down and kissed the top of his head.

This was the last time I would see Don alive.

Fifteen

I TRUSTED YOU, DAMN IT!

A morphine drip can produce some pretty mind-blowing experiences.

I don't know when the IV was inserted into my vein, but it shot me down a rabbit hole and straight into Wonderland. Each of my hallucinations was something different: one included me at the drive-thru window of a burger joint, waiting endlessly and never receiving my fries. Another had me hovering over the entrance to a Michael Jackson concert with Mom and Don waiting to get in. I would have accepted Frank Sinatra, but when you're on a train to Crazytown, you accept whatever comes your way.

The altered world I visited most often placed me on a gurney in an ambulance—or a hospital—with a Middle Eastern female doctor who spoke to me. During all the other adventures, I never spoke, nor did any of the other characters. It was so real, and I entered this realm so often that I wondered if I was supposed to meet her in real life. Rod Serling would have paid good money to include this as an episode of *The Twilight Zone. You are about to enter another dimension...*

Sorry, I never found myself standing before a bright white

light or experienced anyone beckoning me to come toward one. Now THAT would have stirred conversation.

A few months after I returned to the university from the hospital, I called Dr. Henrickson and asked a simple question that had been baffling me: *How did I become sick?*

"You're asking the wrong question," he replied. "What happened in the emergency room is more appropriate."

There was quiet.

Repeating what he said rather than asking, I said, "What happened in the ER?"

"We couldn't pinpoint how or where the infection entered your body, Scott. That's not what you should focus on."

After a shorter pause this time, I took the simplicity of his response as more direction than explanation.

Within a moment after we finished our call—after the polite exchange of wishing each other well—I opened Google and started typing into the search bar:

Medical malpractice attorneys near me.

I eventually found Herrick and Hart, a full-service law firm in downtown Eau Claire, just a short walk from the Eau Claire County Courthouse.

After a phone conversation with attorney Mike Schumacher, I was invited in for a face-to-face meeting.

We gathered in the firm's conference room—an elegant space lined with shelves of imposing law books, framed certificates, and gleaming awards. The décor did its job: I was impressed.

Mike entered moments after I arrived. He had the look of General George Armstrong Custer—minus the goatee—dressed in a modern suit. His well-groomed brown hair, nearly blonde, and his straight, painter's-brush mustache framed a direct, no-nonsense gaze.

"Thank you for meeting with me, Mr. Schumacher," I said, extending the only handshake I could offer—my right myoelectric hand.

"Call me Mike," he said, shaking my hand firmly before gesturing to a chair.

"Yes, sir," I replied instinctively. He smirked, tilting his head slightly.

We each settled into black leather chairs on opposite sides of the long, dark walnut table.

"Walk me through what happened," he said. "Start with your first visit to the ER."

I nodded. "Okay, Mike..."

As he took notes, I told my story as objectively as I could. At times, he paused in his writing, prompting me for more details. Occasionally, he shook his head—sometimes punctuating the motion with a disbelieving, "Really?"

I kept my voice even, stripping emotion from my words as I recounted my experience. I wanted him to see the merit in my case —but more than that, I wanted him to understand me. If he took this on, he wouldn't just be fighting negligence. He'd be fighting for *me*.

When I finished, he set his yellow legal pad and black ballpoint pen aside, folded his hands on the table, and met my gaze.

"We've got a case here, Scott."

A grin started to spread across my face. I bit my lip to keep it in check, then reconsidered and let it grow.

"Let's roll."

No one sat behind the defense. On my side of the room, with the prosecution, sat my entire family. *If only it were a popularity contest,* I thought as I watched the defense's second chair—a frumpy man named Daniel Forbes, dressed in a poorly fitted suit—rifle through the jumble of papers stuffed into his faded leather satchel.

Dr. Junig sat at the far end of their table, buffered by his three attorneys. It had been four years since I'd last seen him. He looked older and slighter than I remembered.

I was feeling rather confident when the call to rise boomed from the front of the courtroom. Judge Thomas H. Barland, a slim, white-haired man with bags that fell like ripples in a lake beneath his eyes, strode into the room. We could all be seated, he said.

It was 9:00 a.m. on a beautiful Monday in Eau Claire, and court was now in session. I resumed my seat in one of the tall-backed, black leather office chairs at our table, straightened the yellow legal pad my attorney, Mike Schumacher, had given me, and settled in for the opening statements.

As the prosecution, we were entitled to go first. In his suave, leisurely way, Mike stood from our table and approached the jurors. With him, he carried thirteen pieces of five-by-twenty-four-inch poster board. He passed one to each juror and to Judge Barland. The jurors looked with wide eyes from Mike to the time-line in their hands, trying not to bump each other as they jostled theirs into a less awkward position.

What they now held was a timeline of my life—beginning when the strep bacteria was first identified and ending with my second surgery on *the bad foot* just months ago.

Compiling these events had been quite the experience for both Mike and me. For him, it was a fact-finding mission that I believe opened his eyes to just how precarious and strenuous my situation had been. One little bacterium was discovered on a Tuesday morning, and by Friday of that same week, many of my major organs had deteriorated to such an extent that doctors deemed me unlikely to survive.

This process led me down a slightly different path. *I had survived;* the degree to which my body had suffered afterward was of little consequence now. The only affliction I cared to acquaint myself with was that of the people who now sat behind me in a show of unwavering support—the people who had stationed themselves outside my hospital room for hours and days on end.

The vivid collection of my family members' individual experiences had mosaicked in my mind to create something far more intricate than a simple chronology of events. As the groundwork for the prosecution and defense's cases was laid, I replayed the stories I had been told, starting with my niece's.

Marie

"I was twelve at the time. Most of what I remember is sitting in the waiting room—just about every day. I knew the hospital hallways like the back of my hand. When the waiting room was full of new people, my mom, Aunt Lisa, and I would sit in the hallway on the floor. I remember someone giving us strange looks because we'd be laughing. Aunt Lisa always tried to keep us laughing.

We'd be camped out on the floor down the hall from your room if we couldn't be in there. And we'd all just hope that laughter really was the best medicine—and that somehow, you'd hear us laughing, pulling for you, hoping for you, and you'd know that you had to keep fighting.

It was the anniversary of the Star Wars movies— so that was the only thing on TV that whole summer. That was the first time I had seen all three, and as silly as it seems, I know that's why I'm so obsessed with the movies now, because something about it was comforting. Watching it with my uncles and brothers … the only thing to keep our minds off what none of us wanted to think about.

And I guess I associate it with the fact that you

made it. I'd probably hate Star Wars if something else had happened."

Both sides played off the same key point during the opening remarks: blood tests.

By Mike, the jury was told that, had blood tests been conducted on my first visit to the ER, the bacteria could have been diagnosed—enabling physicians to begin treatment early enough to possibly save my hands and feet. He referred to me as *Scott* and made sure each and every juror knew who I was and what I had undergone.

Attorney Brad Wentworth, for the defense, was a lanky man with long fingers and a smooth style that reminded me of Mick Fleetwood of Fleetwood Mac—only I pegged Wentworth for a guitarist rather than a drummer. He sauntered to the front of the courtroom in a crisp suit styled just casually enough to be approachable without being inappropriate.

According to him, I was "this unfortunate man," for whom the consequences would have been the same regardless of whether blood tests had been performed by Dr. Junig during my initial visit.

In a detached way, it was fascinating to see how the two attorneys slanted the story—choosing the right phrases, the ideal terms to sway the emotions of the jury.

In reality, sitting in that courtroom, it was irritating to be just an *unfortunate man*. After listening to the way Wentworth cast a verbal shadow over me, I wanted to stand up and parade myself—and each of my family members—before the court. *See me?* I wanted to command. *See my family? Let them tell you how things really were. Then you can determine how unfortunate I am, and what should or should not have been done.*

    Brian
      "On my first trip to the hospital, my brother Chris

and I were waiting in the car for our parents, and he said, 'You know what's going to happen to Uncle Scott, right?' And I just said, 'You don't know that.' I don't really remember much about the whole thing before that, but I do know everyone's mood was pretty low.

When we were finally in the hospital, it was my turn to go see you, and my mom tried to prepare me for what I would see—lots of tubes that breathed for you. Being my usual self, I was trying to crack jokes on the walk to your room, and that was when I knew it was bad, because it just made my mom say, 'Brian!' and she started to cry.

Then we got to your room, and it was much worse than I thought. It looked like you were being raised by a magician—up and down, up and down with the breathing machine. Your eyes were taped shut, but I could still see them, and they were all yellow. Your fingers were starting to turn purple. My mom told me to say something to let you know I was there, and to be loud so you could hear me, but I couldn't really say anything. And when I did, it was just a whisper of, 'Hi, Uncle Scott.'"

When the defense decided to cross-examine my mom, I grinned and scribbled *Mistake!* on my notepad. I tilted it toward Mike, seated beside me, and circled the word. He glanced at what I'd written, and I watched his eyebrows furrow. *He'll understand soon enough,* I thought.

It was the second chair for the defense, Mark Winchell, who was granted the seemingly benign task of interrogating my seventy-year-old mother. I watched the youngest attorney in the courtroom approach the stand and leaned back in my seat to enjoy the show.

Five minutes in, a shine had developed along his forehead,

and his once-fluffy brown hair was beginning to stick to his face. As he continually found himself unable to wrangle this tough-as-nails mother of six, dark sweat stains sprouted beneath the arms of his navy-blue sport coat. Mike jotted something on his own notepad and angled it toward me. I glanced down. *You're right!* was etched on the edge of the yellow paper. He circled it and smiled when I met his eyes, a cocky gleam lighting my expression.

"Your son told the doctor that he was suffering from heat exhaustion," Winchell informed my mother, trying yet again to corner her. His voice was a few decibels shy of assertive and no match for the volume—or the ferocity—of Mom's reproach.

"Scott's not a doctor!" she snapped back. Her whole body seemed to vibrate with indignant fury. There was no way this lioness was going to allow them to pin anything on her cub. "Scott is the *victim* here!" she proclaimed behind her words. "Don't you forget that."

I rocked slightly in my desk chair, basking in the abundance of pride I felt for my mom. Thirty-nine years as her son, and she could still astound me.

As I watched Winchell squirm at her feet, though, my thoughts began to drift. She was on fire—that much was clear—and prepared to fight tooth and nail to defend me. But beneath the flames that sparked menacingly in her eyes was a pain so deep and hardened that not even the light of her fury could mask it fully. In those moments, looking at the strongest woman I knew, I saw everlasting suffering.

Mom
"When you finally got up that Sunday morning, as you entered the kitchen, you got about to the island and threw up—about a gallon of plain liquid. It hit mostly at the sink. That was when I said you had to go back to the hospital.

Shortly after Dr. Ramsey saw you, he said you had to be in the intensive care section because you had a bad case of sepsis and must be watched very carefully.

That's where we met Lindy. She was there and was a wonderful, caring nurse. She finally persuaded me to go home after midnight, promising she'd call if there were any changes. She did call early the next morning, telling me I should call the family—which I did—and everyone came as soon as they could get there. I called my church and had the pastor come for prayers. We were all sitting on the floor in the hall because we were such a big bunch.

It was a few days later when your hands started to turn black. I used to stand by your bed and rub your hands, hoping that would get some life back into them.

One doctor suggested that I should let you go. Of course, I refused to do that."

My back straightened when Mike called Dr. Junig to the stand. Above all else, this was the man I had been waiting to hear from. I knew his answers would only be echoes of what the defense had been parroting all day—but I still couldn't subdue the anticipation I felt as I watched him approach the witness box.

Over the lunch break, my mom had poked her head into the courtroom to find it occupied by Dr. Junig and his team. When she returned to where the rest of us were waiting out the lunch hour in an adjacent chamber, she snidely reported that he was "sitting up there, practicing his answers, proud as a peacock." *Rehearsing won't do this little pheasant much good once Mike gets to him,* I thought, and waited for them to finish their script so the real fun could begin.

The fun, as it turned out, lasted a full hour and thirty minutes. Mike grilled the young doctor relentlessly. Through the research done by the team at Herrick & Hart, I learned that on the day I met Dr. Junig in the ER, he was two days out of medical school. But his young age was certainly no excuse for what his negligence had done to me and my family. If anything, the inordinate amount of responsibility he was given perhaps suggested that the whole of the medical profession should be sitting on that stand beside him.

Though we could have included the hospital in the lawsuit, we went the more simplistic route of targeting one person: Dr. Junig. And one issue: *the lack of a blood test* that would have sent off alarm bells—and those bells would have tripped a much different set of dominoes.

My seat at the prosecution table was situated directly in front of the witness box. I never once took my eyes off Dr. Junig for the duration of his testimony. I hoped sincerely that he could feel the loathing I was casting his way. Because of him, I would forever distrust one of the most benevolent facets of our society—the very people you're meant to trust with your life above anyone else.

I wanted to yell, *I TRUSTED YOU, DAMN IT!* as I willed the mechanical fingers of the myos to clench into fists. *I trusted you, and I almost died.*

And I wasn't the only one feeling betrayed. As Mike navigated his way to the issue of the blood test that was never conducted, Nancy broke.

"Why didn't you check his blood?!" she cried out, her voice desperate and raw. The front of the courtroom turned its collective head to locate the distraught sound.

I felt the flood of my own emotions begin to recede. My feelings meant so little in comparison to those of my family. It was their suffering that cut me deeper than the amputations ever could.

Slowly, I turned my chair just far enough to peer over my shoulder at her. When she realized the attention she had drawn, she folded herself into Jim's open arms, burying her face against his shoulder. I caught a glimpse of tears erupting from her blood-shot eyes before she was hidden in Jim's protective embrace. He nodded to me as he rubbed her quivering back.

 *Nancy*
"One day, when you were in the coma, I came in to visit. I put my left hand on your forehead and my right on your left arm. I felt an electrical shock—with the power of putting my hand in a socket, but without the pain. That's when I knew you were inside that body."

❄

Our expert witness, Dr. Dennis Stevens, was the chief of infectious diseases at the Veterans Affairs Medical Center in Boise, Idaho, as well as a consultant to the Centers for Disease Control on Group A Streptococcus. A man with bright blue eyes and a barren crown, Dr. Stevens offered a timeframe that was more favorable to our theory, citing the "window of opportunity" that Dr. Junig had brazenly denied.

During his cross-examination, Mr. Wentworth blew past questioning Stevens's information in favor of questioning the man himself.

"Dr. Stevens," Wentworth said, his beanstalk body angled toward the jury and his head downcast, a furrow in his brow as if he didn't already know the answer to the question he was about to ask, "how many times, approximately, have you been paid by a plaintiff to sit as an expert witness?"

I scowled. *What does that have to do with anything?*

"Was it more than ten, twenty times?" Wentworth asked coyly when Dr. Stevens sat stupefied for one silent second too long.

"I guess between ten and twenty," Dr. Stevens grudgingly conceded.

I glanced at the jury. Surely, they weren't going to let that small facet of this man's credentials sway their opinion. Dejection swelled over me as I watched the twelve people who would determine the outcome of this case shift in their seats, wide eyes searching for the right person to trust. *They're listening to this lunacy,* I thought, turning pleading eyes to Mike.

On the fourth day of the trial, Judge Barland reported that Juror #7 had fallen ill and could not continue with the trial.

"I hope her temperature is taken and blood tests are run," the judge commented, tongue in cheek.

I bit back a startled chuckle as Brad Wentworth leapt from his chair.

"I object!" he proclaimed in full courtroom-drama style. "Will the court reporter please note my objection—and I would like it documented that Judge Barland's last statement may be used if a mistrial is sought."

Like a classroom where a student has just dared to challenge the teacher, the cavernous room became absorbed in silence—everyone waiting in awe for what would come next.

The judge sighed and shrugged his shoulders as if to say, *Well, if you can't take a joke.* Peering out at the court before him, he acquiesced.

"The jury will disregard my previous statement."

With the matter legally resolved but not forgotten, the trial was resumed. Mike and I glanced at each other with wide eyes. I lowered my head as a grin split across my face.

Jeff

>"Mom called to tell me that you were sick, and that Don had taken you to the emergency room. I assumed you had the flu or food poisoning and went to bed that night not thinking much of it. When she called back the next morning, her tone was very serious. She said that you were extremely sick and might not make it. I left Seattle that afternoon and drove

from O'Hare to Janesville not knowing what to expect.

Walking into the hospital room, I was stunned. Every type of medical machine—not the kind you've seen in person, the kind you see on television—was packed into the room. Devices humming and clicking, screens and monitors everywhere. I said, 'What the hell?!'

Then there you were, in the middle of all the machines. I could barely see you. Mom took me over to you and showed me your hands. They were black and purple, like the worst kind of bruise—all the way up to the wrists. The advancing purple line and the oxygen levels on one of the machines soon became the two things we watched, analyzing and speculating. That, and your eyes. Would you open them at some point? Any flicker of consciousness? At that point, there was none.

Mom took me to one of the doctors who tried to explain. There were far more questions than answers, and for some reason, it seemed possible that the purple line on your wrists might go back down, like the color returning to someone's face after they'd fainted. I don't think the doctor actually said that—we just collectively grabbed onto the notion.

So, the vigil began—mainly Nancy, Denny, Val (Denny's wife), and me—with a rotating cast of others, staring at you and the machines, speculating and telling stories. At some point, I invented the job of crisis manager and took on the task of answering the phone, giving updates to family and friends who were calling as the news spread.

Totally helpless. Nancy, Val, and I were in the room when you first had a little bit of eye movement and seemed to regain a little bit of consciousness. It was pretty sporadic after that, and you certainly didn't come to; but it was an improvement. It gave us hope that we really needed. The downside was that the purple line wasn't going backward—it was advancing. We spent hours watching your eyes and the purple line for any sign."

Tom Peck was called next. He approached the witness box with his eyes up and confidence in his stride. After being sworn in, Mike asked Tom how I had changed after the illness.

"Different," he replied, eyes glancing to the side in search of words to elaborate. "Less outgoing."

The defense came at it a different way. Mark Winchell, who seemed to have recovered from his prior episode with my mom, opened with, "It was unfortunate what happened to your friend, but he has handled the changes quite well."

Tom stared at him.

After a pause, Winchell quickly amended his statement to force a response. "Isn't it true," Winchell asked, "that your friend has been doing quite well in adapting and has, in fact, gained full independence?"

Tom didn't follow the lead. "Scott," he replied, emphasizing my name where Winchell had failed to mention it, "had to work very hard to solve many problems—and he did, but he should not have been placed in a situation to need to do so."

In a flat tone, he went on to inform the court, "Using those hands is quite difficult. I tried to get a better idea of what Scott goes through by wearing stiff mittens for a while... Try it. It's not easy."

Stiff mittens? This was news to me. I was momentarily astounded by the fact that not only had Tom cared enough to try on my perspective, but he had actually found a reasonable way to test it. Then I remembered who I was thinking about—one of the best friends and one of the most intuitive people I had ever known. He, of all people, would take the time to try something like that.

Sixteen

PERCEPTION IS KEY

Week number two of the trial was to begin with me on the stand. Most of my family had returned to their homes during the weekend, but my mother stayed in Eau Claire at a hotel. With another five days of testimony and wrangling scheduled, Saturday and Sunday could not have moved more slowly.

"Hello?" a woman's groggy voice rasped.

"Sue," I said between gasps for air as I cradled the telephone receiver between my head and left shoulder. "This— Is— Scott —" With each word, I felt the loss of more oxygen expelled from my lungs. "I— Don't— Know— What's— Going— On... I think — I'm— Having a— Breakdown."

I heard bed sheets rustling. "Tom will be right over," she said. Now, with a clear and calming voice, Sue continued, "Stay on the phone with me until he gets there." I nodded, realized she couldn't see the motion, and tried to make an affirmative noise.

Sue gave me a moment, then said, "Now focus on your

breathing. Deep, slow breaths, Scott." I heard her draw in a greedy breath of oxygen followed by a slow exhale. She did it again, and I listened hard to the sound of her respiration. As she continued breathing in my ear, I felt my own gasps for air begin to slow. With each new inhalation, the world began to right itself. Shapes stopped blurring, and the black spots receded until I could see everything clearly again.

"Now relax your shoulders as you exhale... good," she soothed.

I could make out the edge of my bed with the sheets rumpled and remembered how I had thrown myself onto the floor in fear, lying with my amputated arms holding my knees against my chest.

"Sit on the floor and find something to lean against if you're not already doing so," she instructed. "Your bed or a wall—something sturdy."

Crumpled on the carpeted floor, I sat upright and scooted myself against the wall for support.

"Scott?" I heard a door close and a man's voice echo up the stairs to me. I heard soft footsteps on the stairs, and then Tom's tall figure emerged in the doorway.

"Hey, buddy," he said when he located me on the floor by the bed. He walked over with soft steps, laying his feet down on the carpet slowly, steadily, as if not wanting to alarm me with any fast motion or loud noise.

I nodded to him as he came to sit against the wall beside me. He then carefully slid the gray receiver away from me and told Sue he had arrived.

"How're you feeling?" he asked as he gently placed the receiver back into its cradle, then sat next to me on the floor. With half my focus still on my breathing, I told him about the heart palpitations and the sweat-coated shakes, the buzzing that had started in my head, and the consuming fear and debilitating paranoia.

I'm losing control, Tom.

"Okay, any idea what might have brought this on?" he asked

carefully, venturing each word one at a time. I said nothing and stared blank-faced at him.

"Well, how about we talk about something else for a while?"

I nodded in agreement.

"The trial seems to be going well," he prompted a moment later, the upward trend of his tone making the statement blur into a question. I nodded again. Tom had attended at least a portion of the trial each day.

"I think it's going in our favor," he continued, stretching his long legs out before him as he turned. "Your mom sure shook up that weaselly defense attorney's world. I've never seen a man sweat all the way through a suit coat before."

I mustered a short, winded chuckle at the thought of my mom staring down the young attorney like a mother with a serious spanking on her mind—and the fact that he looked as if he believed she would do it. I looked to Tom, still smiling at the memory, and he flashed me a grin in return. He was watching me with that wary keenness I was beginning to identify with anyone who had a vested interest in my well-being.

"How about I get us some water?" he asked as he pushed himself to his feet. I nodded and looked down at my own cramped legs. Gradually, I straightened them beneath the bed and rolled my head from side to side to stretch my neck. Then I took a long, drawn-out breath as I reached my arms overhead. I could feel reality beginning to seep back into my muscles, and by the time Tom was back with the water, I was fairly clear-headed.

Tom stayed for close to an hour, and we talked about nothing in particular.

"Thanks, buddy," I said with my eyes locked on his. The side of his mouth quirked upward, and he shrugged one shoulder.

"Nah," he replied. "We're friends."

"Shit!" I blurted as I looked at the clock next to my bed. "I testify in less than four hours."

"You'll do fine," Tom said supportively. "Just avoid being led by their attorney; he's a sneaky son of a bitch."

I exhaled in a prolonged gush of air and smirked at him from the corner of my eye. *No problem,* I thought. *It's my turn to speak about what I've been put through.*

At 9:05 that morning, I obligingly raised my right prosthetic hand and solemnly swore to tell the truth, the whole truth, and nothing but the truth.

Marie
"I remember going into your room while you were still in the coma, seeing machines hooked up. I hadn't seen you much before this. I think that summer was the most time I spent with you, and you were asleep for all of it.

"I remember going in and realizing that your hands looked wrong. And every day they were a little different color, a little worse. And I remember when they were trying to decide what to do about it. It killed every single person to know there was only one choice. But everyone kept hoping and kept spirits up, and it came down to knowing that it was better to have you alive, of course. Everyone was worried you'd be upset. How could you not be?"

❄

Dr. Gene Marsh was the expert witness for the defense. He was a professor at the University of Minnesota and had excellent credentials. His whitening hair was well-groomed, his hands were steady, and he sported a cool smile that emanated experience.

Because their argument was that blood tests on my initial visit to the ER would have made no difference, the logical implication was that an aggressive dose of antibiotics administered early enough would have been fruitless as well. In an effort to demonstrate that time was never on our side, Dr. Marsh was asked to add blue-colored water to a Petri dish to represent the rate at which the toxin in my system grew over time.

As the jury was swooned by pretty colors and smooth talking, I extrapolated the numbers on my legal pad. If Dr. Marsh was to be believed—that each streptococcal bacterium divided every forty-five minutes—the amount of toxic fluid that would have built up in the time between my contraction of the illness and my visit to Dr. Junig in the ER would easily have been sufficient to identify the disease. That is, of course, if Junig had cared to look.

In reality, it had taken days for the infected area in my left flank to be located. The defense, however, was presenting their case as if the clock had started *then*—when the infection was finally found. Sure, by then it was too late; the toxin had spread too deep, and the damage had been done. But if the days it went undiscovered were accounted for, there was no telling what measures could have been taken. It was those precious moments we were in this courtroom fighting over—the moments that decided between life and death, limb loss and total recovery.

I quickly scrawled a note to Mike: *They just proved our case!* He pursed his lips and gave me a pained look. *That may be,* his doomed expression said, *but we have no way of presenting what your numbers mean.*

Mike didn't cry objection, and we didn't try to refute Marsh's testimony with our own expert witness. Instead, Marsh's calculations were allowed to stand in favor of attacking the heart of the matter: incongruity.

During his cross-examination of Dr. Marsh, Mike used an overhead projector to blow up a slide of an article from *Woman's Day* magazine. The article was titled "I Survived the Flesh-Eating Disease." It had been written by a woman named Constance Stapleton two years after my illness and two years before the trial. In the article, Dr. Marsh was quoted as saying, "The GAS organism tends to be localized in bruises or other places with impaired blood flow. There is a window of opportunity—usually three to four days after the onset—when antibiotics can stop the spread. But once the organism causes a significant drop in blood pressure, it becomes much harder to treat."

My blood pressure was recorded as normal on my first visit to the ER. Accordingly, my visit to Dr. Junig would fit into Marsh's "window of opportunity."

As Mike projected the article, Wentworth again sprang to his feet. "Objection!" he cried. I was beginning to hate how quick on his feet the man was. "That's double hearsay, Your Honor."

All eyes turned to Judge Barland, who sat calmly in his chair, his eyes distant, considering. After a period of ostensibly prolonged silence, he asked the bailiff to escort the jury from the room and subsequently had Mike and Mr. Wentworth present their cases to him alone.

I anxiously watched the two lead attorneys conduct a trial within a trial. *He'll side with us,* I thought, watching the judge's cool expression as he absorbed the information. *He has to.*

"Dr. Marsh," the judge called after the attorneys fell quiet.

"Yes, Your Honor," the repulsively cool doctor responded.

"Did you make the statement quoted in the prosecution's article?"

I turned to look at Marsh in the witness stand. He had no choice. He had been quoted in a respectable publication and was now under oath. He had to admit to it. I held my breath.

"I did not."

I stared at him. *LIAR!* I thought with barely concealed vehemence in my clenched expression. *Double hearsay. Bullshit!* I wanted to shout at the judge. *It doesn't change the fact that Dr. Marsh is clearly two-faced scum, eager to pander for whomever cares to pay his fee.*

But for better or worse, I held my tongue and tried to stomach my fury. Two doctors who had betrayed me. At Marsh's denial, Judge Barland dismissed the article as hearsay and had it removed from the trial.

"If we'd had Stapleton, it would have been allowed," Mike hissed indignantly as he resumed his seat. Constance Stapleton would have been able to present a sworn statement that the quote was made by Dr. Marsh to her. Then it would have been her word against his. *I fumed at the galling intricacies of the law.*

A couple of weeks after the trial, I paid a visit to the UW–Eau Claire campus library in search of more information on Dr. Marsh. I uncovered an article from the Health section of *The New York Times* one year after my illness. The title of the article: "A Dangerous Form of Strep Stirs Concern in Resurgence." The subtitle: "Early Recognition Can Save Life and Limb."

I tried not to grind my teeth or pound the table with the side of the myo as I studied the diagram, which was presented with Dr. Marsh as its source.

It was an artistic table comprising three columns. The first listed the days since the bacteria was theoretically contracted. The top cell was labeled *Day 1*, and as you traveled down the column, the count rose to *Day 4*. Beside this was a column titled *Possible Signs*.

In this second column was a short list of the signs and symptoms an infected individual might experience, corresponding to each day. What started as flu symptoms on Day 1 progressed to a fever of over 103 degrees, a severe drop in blood pressure, and blue discoloration of the lips and nail beds on Day 4.

Across the rows for Days 1 through 3, in the third column, was an arrow proclaiming them the *"Window of Opportunity for Penicillin"*—exactly what Mike had tried to argue and Marsh had denied having ever stated.

Marsh's involvement in the article didn't stop there, either. Later, it was written that "The severe group A strep emits some of the most powerful fever-producing substances known," Dr. Marsh said. If an adult has a fever of 102 degrees or higher, "by all means, have a culture taken," Dr. Marsh said. My temperature, as recorded in Dr. Junig's notes from my initial visit to the ER, was 102.8 degrees Fahrenheit.

But it was too late. Marsh had been let off the hook for his contradictory claims, and I had long since progressed past Day 4 —where it was written in column three of his diagram to *"con-*

tinue antibiotics, intravenous fluids, and electrolytes, and remove dead flesh and possibly amputate."

My hands and feet were gone, and I wasn't going to get them back—nor could I fund a manhunt of a lawsuit against the beguiling Dr. Marsh. All I could do was settle for letting bygones be bygones and hope that no other family would ever have to endure what mine had.

Jeff

"At some point, I decided to stay at the hospital. Just in case something happened, good or bad. We didn't know which was more likely. Good news or bad was a fifty-fifty ball. We slept on chairs near your room. I think I was there three or four days and don't recall leaving the hospital.

"I know Mom and I remember the amputation discussion with the doctor differently. Maybe he explained it to her, and then she asked him to explain it again with me there. Here is what I recall: Mom asked me to come with her and speak with Dr. Henrickson. She introduced me as your brother and best friend—I specifically remember that. He told us there were basically two options: try amputation of your hands and feet (at the purple line), which might stop the necrotizing and allow your system to come back online, or begin winding down the life support, which would probably end in you dying. We decided on the spot that you would choose to undergo the amputations. Dr. Henrickson made the other option seem pretty certain—that is, that without life support, in a few days you would be dead.

"It seemed to me that you were trying to hang on. We made our best call, on the fly, standing in that hall with an unsure doctor. I hope you think it was the right choice."

Before the next day of testimony opened, Mike asked me to meet with him in one of the conference rooms down the hallway from the courtroom.

"I'm going to first be calling a psychologist to testify about your mental state and what the future may hold," he said.

I nodded, feeling the blood rush to my face.

"I think it would be best for you not to be in the courtroom. I'll retrieve you after that, okay?" Mike added.

I sat frozen and believe I either nodded or said something to acknowledge I had heard him. I never asked Mike or anyone from my family about what was asked or what was said during the questioning. *I assume suicide was a topic, but I didn't want to know. Avoidance of the truth was how I made it this far. At least that's the trick I played on myself to make it through those first four years.*

Seventeen

A GUN TO MY HEAD

The afternoon sunlight burst through the windows in Tom and Sue's living room. I leaned back in a wooden rocking chair, studying the slice of Domino's pizza I held between the first two fingers and thumb of the right myo, then folded the crust in classic New York fashion.

Tom came back into the room carrying two Cokes. I hastily brought the pizza to my mouth and bit off a chunk. My stomach was wound so tightly that the pizza barely had a taste.

"So," he said as he held one opened Coke out to me, "what now?"

"Mike told me he'd call when the jury has announced their verdict," I replied around my mouthful.

Tom sat on the sofa as he sipped his Coke. "What are Mike's thoughts about it?"

"Without the *Woman's Day* quote to refute Marsh, Mike's at fifty-fifty."

Tom grunted, either in acknowledgment or because of his

own mouthful of pizza. "That's what it all boils down to, doesn't it?"

I nodded and looked down at the strip of crust left in my grip. The attorneys had given their closing remarks that morning. In front of the jury, Mike had said our case was solid, Dr. Stevens credible, and my life not just altered but devastated. The amount of judgment, he informed the jury, should be ten million dollars.

I had squirmed at that number. *Ten million dollars? Maybe my life hadn't been devastated that badly.* But the jurors didn't seem to be bothered by the number he pitched to them, so I had bowed to his professional judgment on the matter.

The second chair for the defense, the plump and frumpy Daniel Forbes, had countered first. "Their request of ten million dollars is so far off we should receive a judgment," he ranted.

I jotted a note to Mike: *Huh?* Mike just shook his head, looking far from impressed by the scattered-looking opposition and his aberrant speech. Wentworth was much smoother when he gave his closing remarks after Forbes; in doing so, he simplified the case to one definable piece: Marsh's testimony.

I turned to look at Tom on the sofa beside me. "Strange how two weeks of witnesses, objections, and arguments come down to an article in *Woman's Day.*"

"Mm-hmm," he said, his eyes on the next slice of pizza. "You know—" He was cut off by the sound of the phone ringing from the kitchen. He turned wide eyes toward me, his hand mid-grab of another slice. I pinched my lips, raised my eyebrows, and nodded.

This has to be it, I thought cautiously.

When the phone cried out a second time, Tom pushed himself to his feet and strolled casually to answer. I could hear the muffled sound of his voice as he picked up. A moment of silence. Then another soft murmur.

He reemerged a moment later, the phone held slightly away from his body as he brought it to me. "Your attorney's on the phone. He says the jury has returned a verdict."

I took a breath, wiped the rubber fingers of my right myo on my pant leg, and stood to take the phone. "Hey, Mike," I said in the best imitation of carefree calm I could muster. My insides were in knots.

"Scott," Mike sighed. He sounded weary. If I hadn't been frozen in place, I might have put the phone down before he could say more. This was not the voice of a man who had just won a battle.

"They came back not guilty," he said. The words flashed through my mind. *Not guilty. Not guilty?* We had lost. I wanted to sit, but my knees refused to bend.

"The jury asked if you could be awarded for limited damages," he continued, "but it wasn't possible."

I looked down at the tracks of pizza grease on my pant leg. With a bent myo finger, I rubbed them, unsure if I was trying to get them out or grind them in further.

"I'm sorry, man," Mike said at length. "We did try."

I swallowed. "Fuck," I muttered. "You did more than I could have hoped for, Mike. Thanks."

When I hung up the phone, Tom was ready with another Coke in each hand. I took the opened one he offered. It was over. The pendulum of my life had swung completely opposite of where it had been before the illness.

Suddenly, my legs buckled beneath me, and I crumpled onto the edge of a cushion on the sofa. I threw my arms out and managed to keep the Coke upright as I teetered forward. Tom grappled for my elbow.

"Easy there," he said, reaching out a steady hand. "You good?"

"Yeah." I slowly set the can back on its coaster. "Yeah, I'm good."

After a few moments of silence, I told Tom I just needed some time to think. He didn't press me, but the expression in his eyes said it all. *Don't lose it,* they begged. *Please, just hang in there.*

I plastered on a smile as I got up to leave; but as soon as I heard the click of Tom's door closing behind me, it vanished. I gasped like a diver coming to the surface and doubled over. It was done. The case was lost. I had nothing. No job. No income. No security. No arms. No feet. No retribution.

I drove in quiet. By the time I pulled into the lower-level garage of my apartment a few miles away, the desperation and dismay no longer felt like they belonged to me. They felt more like distant memories—like emotions experienced vicariously through someone else—not truly my own.

As the door closed behind my car, I chuckled, thinking my friends and family might fear that I wouldn't turn my car off—or that I'd buy a pistol to end it. But I was surprisingly calm as I ascended the steps to the main floor of my apartment.

I passed through the living room and made my way up the second flight of steps leading to my home office. I slid a Peter Gabriel CD into my computer, then stacked other suitable music on the desk for my work ahead: Steely Dan, Talking Heads, Dave Matthews Band, Bonnie Raitt, Traveling Wilburys, Donald Fagen, The Pretenders, Blues Traveler, Bob Marley, John Mellencamp, and Genesis. The soundtracks for the change to come.

As track three of Gabriel's *So* began to rise from the speakers, I opened a fresh Word document. My black Persian cat, Bogart, jumped onto the desk and took his usual perch next to the keyboard. I was so focused on finding a solution to what was next for me that I didn't hear the music—but rather, I let it consume me. I needed to do whatever I could to start the head of the pendulum swinging in the opposite direction. I needed to make it move, because no one else could do it for me.

Eighteen

WESTWARD HO

In numerology, there is a belief in something called a *life path number*: "While each Life Path number carries a unique set of both positive and negative traits, how they manifest is up to you. Life will present you with many chances to flex the muscles of your Life Path number, but you will be the one to choose whether to take the high road or the low road in each situation. The choice you make and the consequences it brings will help guide you in your next decision and so on. Each experience is a lesson in how to become your highest and most authentic self."

My life path number is six. People born with a life path six embrace their emotions and lead with their heart. They give off a warm and inviting energy that others want to be around.

It was time I got back to being that person.

With Bogart draped across my shoulders and my thirty-six-disc portable CD case filling much of the passenger seat to my right, I started rifling through the collection in search of the ideal audio ambiance for the start of our journey. Flipping past disc after disc, I couldn't help grinning at the memories from before the illness. And yes, I had finally moved on from cassettes.

It had been four years and one month to the day since I was first admitted to the hospital—which meant that around this time four years ago, I was just waking from the coma. The realization washed over me like a tidal wave. I sat momentarily frozen in the driver's seat of my car, unable to shake the surge of the past. As it had washed in, the feeling ebbed and pulled back out to sea. But I remembered the pact I had made with myself after losing the trial: *Back to the beginning.*

I blinked to clear my vision and refocused on the CDs. My hand hovered over the sleeve holding Jackson Browne's *I'm Alive* album. A lopsided smile quirked my lips. *Nah,* I thought, and kept flipping past album after album until I came across Tom Petty's *Full Moon Fever.* I slid it delicately out of its pouch and into the deck. "Free Fallin'" came on first. Skip. "I Won't Back Down" came next. Perfect.

"Well, Bogs," I said, "time to hit the road."

We had five states and eighteen hundred miles to cross before we reached our destination—and only three days to do it. I glanced in my rearview mirror instinctively, but I couldn't see anything: I'd filled every available inch of space in my car with my earthly possessions—or at least whatever I had left after a spur-of-the-moment garage sale over the weekend. As part of my purge, I'd chucked every medal, plaque, framed photo, and trophy I'd received during my playing and coaching days into the dumpster of the apartment complex. I was ready to move on.

Between selling, packing, and settling things with my landlord, I had also made the requisite phone calls to my family and friends to break the news of my impromptu move. They had known, as per my game plan, that I'd accepted a position working as an unpaid assistant coach at The Evergreen State College in Olympia, Washington, which would force me to be on food stamps. I knew they thought I was crazy, but I saw it as a necessity. I was breaking myself down so I could build myself back up.

No one had said anything particularly profound to my news that I was heading west—just typical, hasty well wishes and *it's-probably-the-right-thing-to-do's*. As I navigated toward the interstate, I imagined everyone holding a collective breath, anxiously waiting to see what would become of me. For once, singing out Petty's lyrics and cruising down I-94 West, I was breathing easy.

I arrived in Olympia on a Wednesday evening. Though the office of the apartment complex had closed an hour earlier, Maddy, a pleasant lady in her mid-fifties, had left a note on the door to call her—which I did—and she returned to provide me with the key to my modest studio apartment.

I had paid the first and last months' rent after viewing amateurish photos obviously taken with a Polaroid camera. I guessed the person didn't mind being included in the images, given that her reflection appeared in shots of the bathroom vanity, fridge in the kitchen, and other places.

Outside my patio door, which liked to stick when both opening and closing (nothing a little WD-40 couldn't fix), there were cigarette butts, a few expended bottle-rocket cartridges, an empty condom wrapper, and the smell of marijuana in the air. I chuckled as I reminded myself why I was here.

The following morning, I was to meet with the head coach of the men's program, John Wedge, in his office. After so much driving, I needed to stretch my legs, so I arrived early and went on a bit of an exploration mission around the campus. It was beautifully nestled in a forest of moss-covered trees and huge ferns, like nothing I'd ever been able to grow in my college dorm room.

Like a magnet, it didn't take long for my spidey-sense to lure me toward the soccer fields. While walking from end line to end line, I was approached by a man I guessed was in his late fifties or early sixties. He was dressed in a pressed forest-green warm-up with *TESC* on the left chest and *JW* on the right.

Sweet, I thought, noting the classic adidas three stripes along the arms and legs.

"Scott Martin?" he said, jutting his hand out for a shake. "I'm John Wedge. How was your drive?"

As we shook hands, he didn't hesitate—a great sign.

"John!" I replied. "Thanks for bringing me onto your staff."

"I know we're supposed to meet in my office," he said, "but let's go sit on the bleachers and talk."

In the stands, we talked about the ins and outs of the game, and his interest piqued as I told him my views on the importance of commanding the midfield.

"In my opinion, each match is determined by the team that controls the midfield," I responded to one of his questions. "It's more than superior technical play. It's groups of three, four, and five—always having superior numbers by shifting players."

John sat back and tilted his head, pondering inquisitively what I'd told him.

"Tell me more about your use of mathematics in soccer."

John was well known and well respected along the West Coast. Knowing this, we struck a deal that I would join his staff *gratis*, with a focus on tactics, in exchange for his efforts in hitching me up with another college from this region—preferably in a position as head coach.

Evergreen State was an NAIA Division II school and offered no scholarships. As a liberal arts, pass/fail university—and a geoduck as its mascot (*I'll wait here while you Google it*)—suffice it to say I was surprised at the talent of the starting lineup. There was something here to work with.

Later in the year, I sought out a physician to direct me to a professional to begin helping me with *The Fog*—what I assumed was probably called "depression" in a clinical setting.

The year after leaving Wisconsin was crazy. First, the consulting doctor and I got married. This was immediately followed by a call from John Wedge: the head coach of the women's program at Gonzaga University was leaving and had agreed to bring me in as an assistant. The intent was to move me up to head coach with an interim tag after he resigned.

I was excited—this opportunity would allow me to finally gain my footing at a Division I school, one well respected for its academics but not necessarily for its athletics.

In a sudden change of course, the university brought in a new athletics director to boost their sports program. Unfortunately for me, his hire coincided with the coach's departure, and our sand-written agreement washed away into the sea.

But all was not lost. The new director hired me as the assistant to the former assistant, who was now the acting head coach. (*Still following, reader?*) I now had to implement my usually aggressive style while avoiding stepping on her toes.

Though I designed and ran the training sessions, none of my analysis—both pre-match and during play—was considered. It was my worst experience coaching soccer, ever.

By the final match in San Francisco, I totally lost my cool. A freshman player who realized she had left her credentials at the hotel sent me over the edge. She was freaking out. It wasn't even the player that upset me—it was that the head coach was the first person off the team bus and first to check her bags and head to the gate. She was oblivious to the needs of the players.

After calling the hotel to secure the identification and flag down a cab to pick it up and return it to us, I entered the boarding area and ripped into the coach. It felt good to cut loose and finally point out her ineptitudes. Around us, I saw many of the players silently clapping during my tirade. It felt good.

I never heard anything from the athletic director about the incident. In fact, the next week, he asked me to apply for the head coaching position that had since been posted. But little did I know that something else was about to happen that would change my life.

Big time.

Nineteen

TIME PASSAGES

I applied for the head coaching job. There was nothing not to like about Gonzaga. Their women's soccer program played in what was considered the top conference in the country. Their annual home-and-away matches were against two of the best programs in the nation—Santa Clara and the University of Portland, which was led by Clive Charles, whom I personally admired for his work in advancing the game across the United States. Plus, Bing Crosby was an alumnus—and one of my favorite entertainers from the 1930s to 1950s.

The line *"Well, the picture is changing"* from Al Stewart's *Time Passages* set the stage for an evening news report that flipped a switch for me. Back in Olympia between semesters, there was a story on the news about a local family that had adopted a brother and sister from Haiti who had lost both of their parents during Hurricane Georges—two of the more than four hundred people killed.

My wife and I were immediately interested. Within minutes, I began researching adoptions. Romania—a former communist bloc country, like Russia—called out to me. I wanted to speak with someone and learn more, as much and as quickly as I could.

By the time I was headed back over the Cascade Mountains to Spokane from our home in Olympia, our minds were set.

The decision to adopt would mean leaving soccer—the thing I'd come to love more than almost anything else. But I felt clarity. *A clarity like I'd felt while traveling west after the trial.* I picked up the phone and dialed the athletic director at Gonzaga: I wanted to remove my name from consideration. I was tired of fighting the near-constant uphill battle with those who labeled me as disabled.

Of course, the adoption wasn't going to be an easy process—*far* from it. The word *delay* just about sums up the entire thing: delays due to paperwork, delays due to inept accounting, delays due to month-long recesses by the Romanian courts. With my patience as thin as filo dough, I tried to track down a government adoption worker and cut to the chase by offering a bribe. I got connected—only to be disconnected about five seconds later. Strike one.

My next move was to contact the Department of Citizenship and Immigration Services and the Department of Health and Human Services here in the U.S. Strike two.

Next, I wrote to Oprah—why not? It seemed as if she had more power than any government official ever could. Weeks went by without a response, so I called it a foul tip. I was still in the batter's box.

It was time to reach out to our state senator, Patty Murray— once pegged a "mom in tennis shoes" by a male senator after he tried to brush her off—which told me she was the right person to contact. Of course, after writing to her office, it wasn't she who replied but one of her assistants: "I assure you that Senator Murray will move this to the top of her list. It may take a week, but I promise to get back to you."

The assistant called back the next week, and within days my wife and I were heading to Bucharest, Romania's capital. During the flight home with two toddler siblings—a girl and a boy—I began laughing out loud, so much that a flight attendant asked to get in on the joke.

"Sorry," I said with a chuckle. "I can't help but laugh at everything it took to get these guys home."

One year later, I flew to Addis Ababa, Ethiopia, and returned with another son—followed by two more daughters, also from Ethiopia, over the next five years.

Twenty years of parenthood led me to find that children really do grow up. They learn and mature and hit their stride and become full-blown adults. And I also learned—from Al Stewart, and from life—that *the things you lean on are the things that don't last.*

Over the next several years, the seven of us moved from Washington to Colorado, from Colorado to New Mexico, and from New Mexico to Nevada. With each move, my marriage weakened, little by little. After Nevada, we moved once more—back to Washington—where my marriage finally fell apart.

Twenty

SOCCER RATS

As a Little Leaguer at age twelve, our coach invited a friend and former Major League Baseball player to one of our practices. In the days leading up to his arrival, our coach, Mr. Thomas, had only told us that the man had played in the outfield. He had said nothing about him playing in the majors with only one arm.

After a brief introduction, the player approached us to shake our hands. He offered his left hand, catching us all off guard as most of us presented our right hand first, then clumsily switched to our left. But as we watched him rip ball after ball to the corners of our youth field, my teammates and I stood in shock. We started to view him not as a disabled player, but simply as a former baseball professional.

I stood tall on both feet, my weight balanced evenly, hands clasped in front of me. Freshly cut grass fields—reminding me of the Nike complex from nearly twenty-five years ago—surrounded me.

Before me stood a small army of twelve-year-old boys and their families.

Now in Bellingham, Washington, with my two youngest planted firmly in high school and the others either in college or the military, I had spent nearly twenty years as a father and nearly twenty years away from soccer, save some scattered volunteer coaching at my kids' games.

I chuckled to myself and thought about my first youth team in Oshkosh—a team that wore the name of a local realtor, Freid Werner (other teams tagged us as "Fried Weiners"), on the front of our forest-green jerseys. And just like that first team of ten-year-olds—the team that was winless the year before—no one expected much from these kids before me. The Oshkosh team went undefeated during our third season together. *Could I expect the same with this new mangy group? This team of seventeen twelve-year-old boys still a couple of years away from pimples and growing their first whisker? Boys who had already been passed over not only by the top team in the club but the second team, too?*

Never in all my years of coaching youth, high school, and college teams had I inherited a winning team—they'd either been a new startup or were coming off a losing season.

A little girl no older than seven, with a blonde ponytail, tugged on her mother's hand to ask a question. I noticed she was wearing the three broad stripes of blue and red across the right shoulder of a white U.S. Women's National Team jersey—the kit worn during their first World Cup championship. It fit her more like a dress than a jersey, but she seemed perfectly comfortable wearing it.

"Hey, little dude," I said with a smile. "Is that a Women's National Team jersey you're wearing?"

"Yes. It's my mom's from when she was a girl," she proudly responded. She then turned to display the back, which was full of signatures in faded black Sharpie.

"Holy cow!" I was blown away by the names. "I see Michelle Akers, Mia Hamm, Julie Foudy—and my favorite, Kristine Lilly."

"I'm surprised that isn't framed," I said, wide-eyed, to the girl's mother.

"She wears it whenever she can. I have to sneak it away to wash it," she said, looking down at her smiling daughter.

The mother then looked back to me and, with her own broad smile, added, "To me, it *is* framed."

Taking advantage of the icebreaker to address the group, I picked the first boy who stood out—sandy-haired and shorter than almost every kid there, even the younger siblings. His arms disappeared inside a pair of beat-up goalkeeper gloves. The kids weren't even going on the field that day, but he showed up wearing his gloves anyway.

"Matthew MacGregor?" I asked, recalling his name from tryouts.

His eyes widened as he nodded.

"Okay if I call you Mac?"

He glanced at his mom for approval before turning back to me. He lifted his chin a little higher and said, "Sure."

I looked pointedly at his gloves, then met his eyes and nodded.

Next up was a freckle-faced redhead with a side part so deep his bangs swept across his forehead. The only thing brighter than his hair was his distinctive Rave-Green Seattle Sounders jersey. I remembered his cool head and self-confidence from tryouts. By a stroke of luck, the other coaches had passed him up.

"Jack Clement, right?" He nodded in surprised confirmation. "Hair like that needs to be grown down to your shoulders," I told him.

"Cool," he said, then shot a glance up to his folks for approval. When neither objected, his grin widened.

"Tell me," I continued, "what type of position is in your heart, Jack?"

His pale brows furrowed. "What do you mean?"

I looked to his father. "Is he a good student?"

"Yes...?" his dad said—although it came out as more of a question.

"Does he need to be reminded to do his chores? Make his bed? Does he help out without being asked?"

This time there was no hesitancy. "He's a great kid."

Turning back to Jack, I asked, "Do you prefer chess or checkers?"

"Chess. Checkers doesn't do it for me."

"Center back," I told him. "Trust me, that's your natural spot."

Moving down the line, I gave a curly-haired blonde in a yellow Brazilian National Team jersey a hard look. A well-worn soccer ball rested at his feet. I remembered him from tryouts, too; he could link the left to the right and the back to the front of any scrimmage format played. For two days, I'd watched him scan the field at all times, rarely looking down to see where the ball was at his feet.

"Liam Mast," I said, crossing my arms and tilting my head slightly. "Central midfielder," I told him, then added, "Here's the deal: I'm rarely going to tell you what to do, but be ready to answer questions. Got it?"

Liam's mouth gaped slightly, revealing a nice set of braces. I'd just given this soccer rat the golden ticket—freedom to explore. He nodded.

I began strolling slowly across the front of the group again, ready to set the hook. "In fact, boys, in training, I'll have more questions than instructions for all of you. My mission is not to teach you but to put you in a position to learn."

Silence from the crowd. I repeated my coaching mantra as I continued pacing across the intent group: "My mission is not to teach you but to put you in a position to learn. In my observations and opinion, coaches today tend to build robots instead of developing soccer players. With me, you'll learn to play mathematically. You will play as individuals within a team rather than a team that plays as individuals, and you'll learn to turn off your brain and play from your heart."

This time the silence following my words was weighted by intrigue instead of confusion. I'd hooked them now. Like kids waiting to be asked a sure-fire question by their favorite teacher, each of the remaining boys waited eagerly for my assessment of them.

I suppressed a grin. "Chill, guys. I need to watch the rest of you play first." It was rare that three players could walk on the field already wearing their positions as Mac, Jack, and Liam had. "I go by feel," I told them.

My throat tightened on the last word. *It's as good a segue as any,* I thought. *Time to talk about the elephant, the gorilla, and the stinky dog fart in the room.*

Even though the prosthetic hands I now wore looked real at a casual glance, without wrists—and being a person who talks with his hands—they could become a distraction, especially to twelve-year-old boys. I hated being reminded of my disability, but I always understood the curiosity.

The years and experiences since the illness had given me the chance to come to more than a few conclusions. I needed to view times like this as opportunities to step forward on behalf of everyone who stands out in the crowd for a perceived negative condition.

Settling myself on top of the picnic table, I first asked everyone to call me Scott. "We're going to be working together, boys, so please address me as Scott."

I took a breath and said the words I'll never get used to saying: *"Let me tell you about my disability."*

Twenty-One

SETTING THE TONE

I met Richard Peters, the club's director of coaching, in his office—which was largely empty, save for a metal desk and two chairs. Along one wall, painted a stark white and void of any photos or mementos, lay several white mesh bags of soccer balls. Leaning against another wall was a large whiteboard with the outline of a soccer field and twenty blue and red magnets representing the field players, plus two green ones for the goalkeepers and one black one for the ball. I noticed that the magnets were set as two teams—one in a four-four-two formation and the other in a one-four-three-two. *Very defense-minded,* I thought.

I stood in the doorway of Richard's office for what seemed like several minutes before he finally looked up and spoke.

"Steve Martin?" he questioned.

"No, that's my uncle," I quipped with a chuckle. "It's Scott."

He ignored both my correction and my joke, gesturing for me to sit in one of the gray metal folding chairs in front of the desk. Placed prominently on his desk was an award for Coach of the Year from five years earlier. *Note to self: avoid mentioning the four such awards I've earned.*

Richard looked at me oddly. He never offered to shake hands.

In fact, he seemed to avoid looking at my hands altogether as I clamped them around the knee of my crossed leg. I didn't want to break the silence first, but I couldn't help it.

"How was your move from—where was it, Indiana?" I asked. Ice successfully broken.

He filled me in on everything—too much, maybe—from picking up his U-Haul rental outside Indianapolis to dropping it off in downtown Bellingham. Not once did he ask me about my own venture, which was fine by me. The meeting was shaping up to be as boring as a gathering of bankers at a paperclip convention.

"So, we're happy that you'll be taking over the U-13 boys' C-team," he said when he was done storytelling, with what seemed to be an honest smile.

"So, the 'C' means...?" I began to ask.

"The lowest level."

My eyebrows shot upward.

I arrived at Field 8 of the soccer complex thirty minutes before our first training session. We were the last to be assigned a field. The A and B teams had already trained twice before my boys had even set foot on grass. I was champing at the bit to get started, but the delay at least gave me the chance to see how training sessions had changed since I was last in charge at the youth level.

As I walked from session to session the week before, one thing stood out: there was too much lecturing and too little play. The coaches had their players harnessed like plow horses, running from colored disc to colored disc. So many discs—littered across the fields like someone had dumped a giant box of crayons and said, *Go!*

One thing I learned coaching in Europe was that drills were for practicing skills, but teams were built during competitive play —especially during training. I wanted to give my players the room to explore, to experience this beautiful game. To me, soccer was more an art than a sport. It was abstract expressionism—perfectly imperfect when played from the heart. Like a Jackson Pollock painting, where many may see no rhyme or reason, others see the flow. *I see that same flow in the game of soccer.*

In the very first training session I ran as a college freshman, I rolled a soccer ball onto the lush grass and told the kids, "The ball is your brush, and the field is your canvas. Paint a beautiful picture."

I walked onto the field, finally available, to find it already occupied. A man of medium build in a black adidas cap was standing in the center circle. Sunlight glinted off his eyeglasses as I approached.

"Phil?" I asked, extending a prosthetic hand to greet my new assistant coach's flesh-and-blood one.

"Yeah. Great to meet you," he replied, gripping the prosthetic hand without pause.

Having prosthetic hands gave me an advantage when sizing up others. If they hesitated or flinched, it told me they lacked confidence. I loved greeting opposing coaches before a match to throw them off a bit and assess their position. I was glad to see Phil pass my confidence test with flying colors.

As usual, I brought very little equipment with me that day. All I needed for our session fit neatly into a gray, water-resistant backpack: twenty-five blue and white discs (though I planned to use very few, after what I'd seen the week before), ten yellow and ten blue pinnies, a small air pump and needles, Wrigley's Spearmint gum, and my green tubular Bluetooth speaker. I set the bag on the kickoff spot and went over the plan with Phil.

Soon, small SUVs and minivans began pulling into the parking lot. As the boys trickled onto the field, I gave the incoming band of castoffs another once-over. They ducked out of cars and scurried onto the grass. Most of them kept their eyes on the balls at their feet. Even Liam—who I knew could run a ball across the state without looking down—kept his eyes lowered as he joined the others clustering near Phil and me.

A few waved to each other, but the greetings were short-lived.

Their eyes darted back to the balls at their feet as they waited for me to begin. They looked guilty, as if they didn't think they belonged.

Despite that, I was proud to see that not one of the boys had carried his ball onto the field with his hands. They all used their feet.

"I think we have something to work with," I said to Phil.

"Get a load of their jerseys, too," he said.

As was the norm in the early season, equipment for the club had been delayed, so the players were still in their personal gear. The boys' jerseys spanned the globe: Barcelona, Manchester United, Arsenal, Germany, Brazil, Colombia.

"Look—one kid's wearing a Santos jersey with Pelé on the back," I said, clapping Phil on the shoulder with a grin. "The other coaches screwed up by not selecting these kids for the upper teams. These are soccer rats."

At six o'clock on the dot, I began our first training session.

"All right, guys, before we get started, let's get something straight: be brave enough to suck at something new. If you don't make mistakes, you're not training properly. And for goodness' sake, leave your male egos on the sideline.

"Capisce?"

To my surprise, all of the guys called out, "Capisce!" in unison. *I was going to have fun with this scruffy group.*

"How many days are left in the school year?" I asked as we walked to one end of the field.

"Eight," Jack said.

"Ah, man, we have twelve because of the extra snow days," said another.

"I'm finished," Isaiah said from right beside me.

"That sucks! Why do you get off?"

"I'm home-schooled, and my mom always stays ahead of

schedule. You won't have to worry about me ever being late, Scott."

I glanced down at the top of Isaiah's head. Medium brown hair curled out above his ears. He'd attached himself to my side like a little soldier. *Not surprising, given what his mom had told me about his previous coach.* Isaiah's last soccer coach was the type of guy who fancied himself more drill sergeant than coach. Nick held back a bit. Ryan even further.

"Always remember that your studies come ahead of soccer," I told him. "But, yeah, that does kinda suck for the rest of you guys —especially the snowbound dude."

Next came a question that told me the boys were already becoming comfortable with me.

"Hey, Scott?"

"Hey, Isaiah," I said as I came to a stop to allow Nick and Sawyer to catch up.

"You don't seem disabled. How hard was it to learn to redo everything?"

An educator at heart, I knew a learning opportunity when I saw one. I also knew the need for the boys to get over the hump of my disability and really view me as normal.

"Can any of you guys bend a soccer ball around a wall of defenders?"

The guys paused and looked around for someone to accept my challenge. No takers emerged.

"How big of a wall?" Jack finally asked.

I smirked. "Five players."

Someone whistled at the difficulty of putting a ball on target after getting it around such a wide group of opponents.

"To learn how to use these babies," I said, lifting the prosthetic hands, "I did the same thing I did to learn to bend a ball. I accepted that failing is part of the process."

"If you don't make mistakes, you're not training properly," Sawyer chirped in.

"Exactly, Sawyer," I smiled. "Now let's get to work."

After dynamic stretching, I sent the guys on a light jog around the field to allow them to chat and release their final butterflies. When they completed their lap, we gathered in a twenty-by-thirty-yard area I'd marked with blue discs in ten-yard increments.

"We'll begin with individual defending and progress to larger group defending," I told them. "One step at a time. *Learn, and you move forward.*"

I gestured to the middle of the grid where a soccer ball waited. "See that stupid little round thing we call a soccer ball? Now, look at all the grass. Once we know where the ball is, we limit the ability of our opponent to use the green area. After the ball, the most important thing to control is space. At every level—even the pros—most players focus on the ball and don't see the field. We're going to use that to our advantage."

I moved the team through individual defending drills, then expanded the amount of pressure to three-versus-three games in a larger grid. Limiting space remained the main objective, but in teams, we added intercepting passes into the mix.

"The initial goal isn't to steal the ball," I told them. "We first need to slow progress. *Then* we can coax our opponent in the direction that's least threatening to us. It's a patience game: eventually, they'll feel the need to pass the ball. That's when we take it back."

The boys jumped into the drill with enthusiasm, clearly eager to show off and please. But enthusiasm quickly waned as things skewed off the path.

"You're supposed to pass the ball!" Cache burst out after a few minutes, his voice pitched with frustration.

"Why would I pass it when I know you're just going to steal it when I do?" Jack shot back.

"Because that's the whole point of the drill! We can't complete the drill until you pass."

"The point of the drill is patience. Didn't you listen to Scott?"

Other boys stopped their games at their teammates' raised

voices. I stepped over to their grid before things escalated any further. "Hey, time out. Let's take a breath."

Cache exhaled like a bull seeing red.

"Chillax, dude," I said with a smile. "It's not supposed to be easy. If it was, we wouldn't need to practice it."

"But he's not cooperating," Cache said, still frustrated.

"And you expect your opponents will?"

Cache kicked at the grass. He mumbled something that sounded like a *no*.

"Instead of focusing on your goal of intercepting the pass, think about it from your opponent's perspective. Use his objective against him. Keep denying him forward progress until he gets so frustrated that he wants to pass."

"But it isn't *working*. He's not cooperating."

"It will. Get inside his head. Get creative."

"Yeah, man, get inside my head," Jack taunted playfully, weaving his head back and forth.

Cache started to grin. "Ah, man, I don't want to know what goes on in there."

"What are you talking about? Magic happens in my brain. It's like a magical forest."

Cache snorted. "Just play the ball."

Ten minutes later, things suddenly clicked. I could see the dominoes begin to fall as frustration gave way to patience and desperation to assurance that eventually the ball would be exposed. The first step of their progression had taken place. *Now it's time to work on their flow as a team.*

"Okay, gentlemen," I said, drawing their attention. "This is my backyard, and you've been invited to play soccer. No whistle. No direction. This is 'old-school' soccer. But what I'm going to expect from you is very difficult: I want each of you to turn off your brain and play from your heart."

It was a refrain they'd hear again and again over the next six months—something I'd repeat at every opportunity because I knew from experience how hard it was to get it right.

"Turn off your brain and play from your heart," I said again.

Not waiting for anyone to ask a question, I tossed blue pinnies to eight players and yellow pinnies to eight others. Isaac, left without one, ducked his head and started slinking back to the edge of the group. From a very large, racially mixed family in whitewashed northwestern Washington, Isaac was no stranger to being overlooked.

I called his name, and his head shot up. "You, sir, are going to play the plus-one position. You'll always be on the team that possesses the ball. You good with that?"

A huge smile overcame him. "Sure am!"

He stepped forward as the other boys told him how lucky he was.

I stepped over to my backpack to link my phone and trusty portable speaker. The music wasn't for the players but for me—to use as a metronome to set their pace of play and creativity. I turned up the volume on "Howlin' for You" by the Black Keys and popped a stick of Wrigley's into my mouth as the boys took their first step in playing free-flowing, self-directed, artistic soccer. Phil and I just stood there and watched.

The boys edged farther onto the field. They cast glances at each other, waiting for someone to take the first step.

"You'd think they'd never played a game before," Phil murmured.

"Probably haven't played one that wasn't micromanaged," I replied. *If their previous coaches were anything like the ones I'd seen these past weeks, these boys had probably never been granted this much freedom on the field.* I whistled and waved for them to come together again.

"When I was a kid," I said, "we had the biggest yard in the neighborhood and hosted everything from baseball to soccer on it. Imagine this is my yard, and there are no coaches around to stop your game. Go play some backyard soccer."

They scattered again. At first, they ran the ball back and forth as if they were playing in swimming lanes instead of a wide field. But gradually, pass by pass, they began to turn off their brains. Their movements became free; the space they occupied wider. By the end of training, I could see the beginnings of a Pollock painting taking shape beneath their feet.

I grew up with American soccer when it depended on clubs, primarily in the larger cities. In our region, there were the Croatians and Bavarians in Milwaukee, the English clubs out of Madison, and the Poles and Irish in Chicago. A slew of first- and second-generation ethnic clubs stretched south into St. Louis. All the big clubs had youth divisions that depended on their kids aspiring to play for the top team, like their fathers and uncles had done before them.

During my time, we could watch foreign players like Franz Beckenbauer, Johann Cruyff, Giorgio Chinaglia, George Best, and Pelé finish their careers making good money in the North American Soccer League. The league died due to poor planning and bad management, but it did jump-start the game in the U.S. And the creativity of its players inspired a bunch of kids in central Wisconsin—kids like me.

The Wisconsin Rapids Kickers were started by Klaus Kroner, a first-generation player from Germany. A high school German teacher by day, Klaus spent his after-school hours promoting soccer among the locals. Recruit by recruit, he built a team of soccer rats and misfits (mostly German immigrants, with a few white-bread Wisconsin natives like my brother and me mixed in) who cared deeply for each other—and cared deeply about winning. At sixteen, playing with and against experienced men in their twenties and thirties, it was sink or swim.

Klaus expected us to play freely and creatively and pressure the hell out of our opponents. Our gang of mutts won back-to-back league titles, once even going undefeated. Though I went on to be part of three straight titles with the Pepsi Spirits—who had more individual talent—the Kickers won by playing *for* each other.

You can probably guess the direction I was going to take these boys.

A shadow appeared beside mine on the soccer field. I turned to see Richard Peters, my boss, a bulky man who compensated for his average height by lifting his nose at every opportunity. He came to stand next to me on the edge of the field. He shoved his hands into the pockets of his black adidas windbreaker. Richard still wasn't one for shaking hands—at least not mine.

"How are things going?" he asked.

"The boys are soccer rats," I told him. "They enjoy playing and learning. I think the evaluators missed on a few, and I'm happy to have them."

"Well, this is a C-team. Stay with the basics. We need numbers to keep the club running."

I didn't reply. After a moment of silence, he turned and walked to the adjacent field and another team.

When the scrimmage ended, Phil came over to ask what Richard's visit was about. I just shook my head. "Let's embrace the role of Cinderella."

"No respect, huh?" Phil said.

"Nope. At least we won't be bothered by upper management." I took Richard's visit as a sign that we were free to do things my way. And my way was creative, free-flowing, downright entertaining soccer—the way it was *meant* to be played.

As the boys brought the discs back to Phil and me, Luke paused beside me. He brushed sandy hair from his face.

"Scott?" he asked. "What was the most difficult thing about being in the hospital—the food or not being able to leave?"

I recognized the question for what it was—a softball curved around what he really wanted to know about: my independence. A leggy kid with fast feet, Luke had shown some of the best technical skills on the team. The kid could go far with the game if he was willing to put in the work.

"Actually, the food wasn't half bad," I told him honestly. "The people were great. But it was a lot of work, Luke. Like training to win matches. A lot of hard work."

The following week, Luke started staying late to work on his technical skills while his father waited in the family minivan.

Twenty-Two

GRIEF, ACCEPTANCE, PROCESS

After my initial release from the hospital and return to the Eau Claire campus, Sue Peck handed me a small pouch of tarot tiles and asked me to select three. After realizing that I was unable to reach into the bag myself, she placed each of the twenty tiles upside down on the table in front of me, from which I selected three.

"So, these'll give me insight into my future, right?" I asked.

"As well as the past and present," she said, acting as my spiritual advisor. "Overall, they are a reflection and provoke thought."

She flipped the first over:

GRIEF

Then she flipped the second:

ACCEPTANCE

We both looked at each other with raised eyebrows. "That's interesting," I said, then flipped the third and final tile over.

PRAYER

"What do you think about that one?" Sue asked.

"I don't think praying is what I need," I sighed.

"Okay—consider the term *process* instead," she added.

I nodded. "That makes more sense. *Process.*"

Part of my belief in developing players in a team environment was placing them under pressure through competition. I approached the other U-13 coaches to see if they'd like to set up scrimmages between our teams.

The coach for the A-team gave me a sneer wrapped in a pitying, *thanks-but-no-thanks* smile. No way did he want his "top-level" players scrimmaging against the lowly C-squad.

The B-team coach was more receptive. Jose's players were the middle children of the age group; they didn't fit the mold for the A-team but were still deemed a cut above my guys.

These second-level players were larger and started the summer only a bit higher on the technical scale, but I wanted my guys to be tested as often as possible. *Improvement happens by taking one step backward followed by two steps forward.*

Every Wednesday evening, Jose and I greeted each other at the kickoff spot of the field we shared to discuss the current status of our teams and joke about life. Not once did Jose flinch when shaking my hand, nor did he inquire about my disability. It was refreshing to talk soccer as colleagues, with nothing clouding the air between us.

When a club offers more than one team per age group, players tend to follow the pecking order. They play according to which team is supposed to be superior. In our first scrimmage, the B-team pressured my guys from the opening whistle.

I acted as referee on the field, leaving Phil to manage the players. I said nothing to the boys as the B-team scored on us again and again. And again. And again. And again. And again.

I blew the final whistle. Final score: 0–7.

"Had your butts kicked today, huh?" I asked when we'd gathered on the side of the field.

"Who was the team that kicked your butts?"

"That was the B-team, Scott," Lucas said.

Crossing my arms over my chest, I paused long enough for heads to begin to rise from their dejected stances.

"No," I said. "That was another team from our club. There is no difference between them and us. I suggest you stop playing the role of third-level players and change your way of thinking. I'll see you tomorrow."

Contrary to my coaching career, I had never played on a losing team. It wasn't luck from whistle to whistle of each match but rather the work and camaraderie among teammates during training that made the difference. Individual skill went only so far.

Into our second week of training, I started playing music from my Pandora station right away. With the volume cranked on "Night Train" by Tab Benoit, I popped in a stick of Wrigley's and called for the boys.

Missing one player, I told them, "Divide into four teams of four." I then continued, "You have five seconds." Limiting the time kept them from forming by default into groups they were comfortable with.

Once teams were formed, I said, "Welcome to my backyard. Two teams in different pinnies in each twenty-by-twenty-yard grid. One ball. No goals. Brains off. PLAY!

I let the guys go for a full ten minutes, stopping them only once to fill them in on a little secret. "Soccer can be played at more than full speed. When a team is in sync, they can force their opponent to chase the ball—like a game of musical chairs. Do it right, and your opponent will be the one left without a chair—or the ball. Change things. Be creative. It's okay to make mistakes."

As play resumed, there was a marked difference. I turned to Phil.

"Notice the flow of play. We're beginning to see a rhythm. Next, we'll work on their math skills."

Although UW–Oshkosh only offered soccer as a club sport, as a freshman, I had entered the broadcast journalism program, joined hall government, and the men's soccer club. Professor of Sociology Jerry Stark, who was also the president of the Oshkosh Youth Soccer Club, coached the team and knew that I had played up front as an attacker. But during our first training session, Jerry changed my view and deepened my love for the game with three words: *Run the defense.*

With that challenge, he released a desire in me to dissect the game and evaluate how it should be played. Along with my daily schoolwork, I visited the library and took notes on what I saw on video from the top professional and national teams. Perhaps my greatest takeaway was how mathematics played a role in the use of angles, percentages, and probabilities.

Early into my research, an image began to take shape from my video reviews. I grabbed a notebook and drew eighteen-yard lines that ran at forty-five-degree angles outward from each goalpost into the penalty box. I connected these lines with an arc that touched the top of the arc outside the box. Turning back to the videos, I plotted every missed shot in red and every made shot in green from various matches.

What I found blew me away: the number of shots needed to score inside my plotted area was fifteen times less than the shots taken to score outside the area.

I sat back and stared at my notebook. *We need to focus on defending and attacking this "Scoring Zone."* What went on inside the SZ would become the base of my coaching philosophy.

The next day, I introduced the boys to angles and percentages. Playing more creatively, we began to expect passes and runs to be made into space at angles—anything from greater than zero to one hundred eighty degrees. And by reducing the angles available to an opponent, we limited the percentages for them to score.

I gathered the team inside what I called the "D"—the arc at the top of the penalty box that designated the ten yards defending players needed to stand away from a penalty kick. I'd marked the Scoring Zone with blue discs. Having built a team website full of important information, phrases, and my Ten Principles of Play, I rattled off questions to check their knowledge.

"Is the percent of goals scored higher or lower inside the SZ?" I asked.

"*Higher!*"

"By forcing our opponent wide, what should we expect them to do the closer they get to the end line?"

"*Serve the ball into the Scoring Zone!*"

"Which is more dangerous to the defense: an angled run and pass or a straight run and pass?"

"*Angled run and pass!*"

"Excellent," I said, pleased to see they'd grasped the concepts. "But based on your play, you haven't truly learned how to apply the simple math of the game."

Isaiah spoke up. "But, Scott, how are we supposed to play mathematically if you tell us to turn off our brains and play from our hearts?"

I smiled. "Finally, you're comfortable enough to ask that question. You're going to learn the math of the game through repetition. We have three weeks to understand it so well that you won't need to think about it. Accept that you're going to make mistakes. When you've done this, you'll be ready to play from your hearts."

As the boys jogged to collect their soccer balls, I called for Isaiah to hang back. I'd noticed him struggling more than the rest with our 'backyard' style of play. He often spent more time glancing at me on the sidelines than watching the ball, the space on the field, or the other players—so he was always scrambling to catch up.

"What was training like with your old team?" I asked him.

He scrunched his eyes. "I dunno. A lot of drills, I guess. Mostly drills."

"Did you scrimmage during training, too?"

"Sure, but we always had assigned positions."

"So, you knew exactly where you were supposed to be and what you were supposed to do."

"Yeah."

"But when we play here, everyone is free to play based on an understanding of our team's shape and the situation."

His eyes brightened. "Yeah. Exactly! I don't know where to go."

"How about instead of trying to go where your position tells you to be, go where the situation tells you to be?" I suggested.

He pondered this for a moment, then nodded. "Okay. I'll try."

I nodded in return. "Good. That's all I can expect. Remember, it's okay to make mistakes in training. Try new things and accept failure, then try and succeed—or possibly fail again. Keep trying until you get it right."

As he jogged back to join the others, I switched on Jack White's *I'm Shakin'* as training continued to the beat of the blues rock. Getting players to feel comfortable making their own decisions was perhaps the most difficult hurdle to overcome.

Match Day finally arrived as the boys fidgeted on the unfamiliar field in Tacoma, the location of our first tournament. They stood in a tight cluster, casting surreptitious glances at the other team they'd be playing. It was our first tournament of the summer and the first time they'd be playing someone other than the B-team or each other. Nerves buzzed around them like a swarm of bees.

While they had a good handle on the basics of ball control, proper defending, and managing their pace during a full match, there remained a lack of confidence among them. They weren't sure they belonged yet. Luckily, we had five tournaments and nearly three months to boost their confidence before state league play began.

I pulled them into a circle. "Who's nervous?" I asked.

Everyone's hand went up. A good sign.

"So am I," I said. "Avoid going behind the bench because I puked back there."

A few jaws dropped.

I smiled. "Don't be dweebs. Of course, I didn't throw up," I admitted, which got everyone laughing. *Mission accomplished.*

Normally, I let my players prepare themselves mentally for a match in whatever way they choose. They could knock a ball around, jog with earbuds, or gather their teammates to play a casual game of keep-away. For our first tournament, though, I wanted them to learn something about analyzing an opponent. An opposing coach will often provide a glimpse into their style of play by what they have their players do before a match.

I had the guys gather on the sideline to watch the other team warm up. The players ran from one yellow disc to another and back again, striking or passing the ball as instructed by the coach.

"What do you notice about these guys?" I asked my boys.

"They look like robots," Jack said, pushing his bangs off his forehead. True to his word, he was letting his hair grow and would soon be sporting a nice red-headed shag. "None of them are playing the ball with their left foot. Let's force them to play to their weakness."

"Great analysis," I said. My group of misfits was learning the game. "They just gave you the gift of information. *Use it.*"

From the first whistle, the boys played with patience and at dual speeds, playing fast when we possessed the ball, then slowing down the opponent's progress when they had it. They'd become adept at our defensive philosophy of not trying to steal the ball. Rather, we tried to maneuver the opposing player into a position where his options were limited. Then we intercepted and quickened the pace. The objective was always to play with our hips facing the opponent's goal while they chased us.

And chase us they did. Just minutes into the game, Isaac got control of the ball. He ran it down the right flank, almost to the end line. At the last moment, he served it to Nathan, who sent it straight into the back of the net.

It was the first goal of the game and our first goal as a team in a full match. But you'd never guess it watching Nathan. As the other boys whooped in celebration, Nathan ducked his head and jogged back toward center field. This was his modus operandi: do something impressive, then pretend it never happened. As if he thought it was all luck and no skill on his part, and therefore not worth taking pride in.

I hoped that if he learned to trust me as his coach, he'd also learn to believe in himself as the talented player that he was. There was the making of a top goal scorer in that kid. I just had to convince him of it.

With self-confidence comes a willingness to push the bounds of what you can do. The old adage, "you never know unless you try," hinges on the fact that we'll only try if we think we stand a chance of success. No one embodied this better than Mac, our pint-sized aspirational goalie.

At twelve years old, it's not uncommon for players to want to play goalkeeper. I had four such kids on this team, including Mac. Richard asked me to limit it to two, but I refused. At this age, there should be no specialization in any one sport or position. And at twelve, no one—not their coach and certainly not a club administrator who spends more time in his clubhouse than on the field—has any right to tell them who they can or cannot become.

My intention for tournament play was to rotate our goalkeepers at each half, with the top keepers playing more if the team progressed into the playoff rounds. Since Mac had yet to establish himself as our top keeper, he played on the field, too. It didn't surprise me to see him strike a halfway-decent bicycle kick as the first half ended. The ball bounced off the crossbar, but we still entered halftime up 1–0. Phil and I chuckled with pride at our team daredevil.

Twelve is old enough to skip halftime "fun" and sliced oranges. Our players jogged off the field and headed straight for a place to sit and rehydrate. After three minutes for the boys to unwind and joke a bit—especially after Mac's attempted bike—it was time for Phil and me to talk. I kept it short. A coach should never speak for more than two of the five minutes that make up halftime in most tournaments. One minute was my usual target.

"What's the score?" I asked.

"0–0," they chorused.

I nodded. Often, young players will either tense up when in a difficult situation or relax too much when ahead. I'd told my guys to always view the score as being 0–0 until the final whistle was blown.

"Here's what I see from the opponent's perspective: you're changing pace, controlling the ball, and limiting their options. Well done. You have them on their heels. Now knock them on their asses."

Jack controlled the back line, Liam managed the midfield, and Mac was acrobatic in the goal. The boys closed things out at 4–0.

After the match, it took a bit more time than I'd have liked for the players to settle. I understood their excitement—it being their first match, and a win to boot—but I also noticed an issue during the game that needed to be nipped in the bud.

When there was a lull in the revelry, I cleared my throat for their attention. "Cocky is good," I told them. "Arrogance is bad. Understand what you did well, but don't overlook what needs improvement. Think about that."

I knew that if I took the reins and controlled their emotions now, whatever the boys learned from their second match would be wasted. Sometimes kids need to learn lessons firsthand through a bad experience to make the lesson stick.

And my instincts were right.

We played too casually in our second match, and the boys paid for it.

Our opponents scored on us in the first two minutes. When a second goal slipped past Mac, the boys began to play out of frustration. Down by three, they started playing out of desperation. I didn't intervene. They'd learn.

Heading into our final group match of the tournament, I laid it out for the boys: "We need to win by three goals to play again. Trust me to manage the match."

I scanned their faces to find them focused on my every word. Knowing I had their faith, I simplified matters by reminding them of one key thing—my broken-record mantra: "Turn off your brains and play from your hearts."

Throughout the match, all the guys pressured the ball when it was at the opponent's feet. We dominated, taking a dozen shots within the other team's scoring zone, while they managed only one shot against us from well outside ours. Frustration and desperation appeared to have switched sides. We won 5–0 and advanced to the playoffs.

Anyone who has experienced competitive youth soccer knows that tournaments can be rough on the entire family. Parents often play tag team—driving and hauling lawn chairs, sunscreen, and drinks to and from the fields—and entertaining younger siblings who are constantly in search of their next snack or dandelion to pluck. And Lord help those with another kid or two playing on a different team—seemingly always at the same time and on different ends of the complex.

Of course, advancing into the playoffs was grueling for the players, too. Having played a match on Friday evening, both teams were entering their third match of the day as the evening began on Saturday. We were about to see how well my boys had learned to manage their sprint steps, avoid greasy foods, and drink plenty of fluids.

Immediately after the opening kickoff, our opponent strung together three quality passes and entered our scoring zone. Their top player, sporting a fresh spiked haircut, took a shot as Jack attempted a slide tackle. The ball zinged off his left foot, heading toward our goal. Mac jumped into the air, but there needed to be three of him stacked one on top of the other to stop this one. Luckily, the ball was on an upward arc and bounced off the cross-bar. Jack headed it clear, and everyone let out a collective "Whew!"

We returned the favor, ringing a ball off the opponent's goal-post. Then another. And another.

Despite the boys' solid work at slowing down the play while the other team had the ball, our opponents still managed to take three more shots against us. None of them made it past Mac.

Having scoped out the tournament scoreboard, we found that although our opponent had won all three of their matches during group play, they'd done so with only one goal in each game. Couple that with this tight match, and I saw the brick wall of fatigue in their near future.

Luke had played fewer than twenty minutes this match and was fresh. The opposing right back had yet to rest. It was time to release this hound.

"As the old saying goes, get chalk on your cleats. Pull him wide and look for a ball played behind him," I advised Luke.

"Get caught offside, and you're dead meat—got it?" I added with a smile.

True to form, with two minutes to go, Liam slotted a ball behind the fatigued right back in stride for Luke, who no longer had to worry about anyone behind him. It was him and the charging goalkeeper, who was now five yards away from his goal. Luke flicked his left foot to the center of the six-yard box, where a jogging Nathan tapped the ball across the end line.

Final score: 1–0.

With our quarterfinal win ending after 8:00 p.m. Saturday night, everyone was ready to kick back for a group dinner and a few beers for the parents. (I limited myself to one. Okay, fine—two.) After I left our hotel restaurant at 10:00 p.m., many of the parents stayed behind.

With many of the parents behind dark sunglasses and deep in their lawn chairs for our early morning match, we went up 1–0 on a perfectly placed thirty-yard serve from Sawyer's left foot to Jugraj's head that ripped into the back of the net.

"Nice start!" I shouted to our non-starting group.

Much of the remainder of the match was played in the middle of the field. But late in the game, a ball was played behind Jack, who slipped during his turn. Their center attacker played one-on-one with Mac before laying the ball past his outstretched hands for the tie. Regulation time ended in a deadlock.

Two five-minute periods awaited us. Twice, Isaac locked his radar on Nathan's head at the top of the six with perfectly weighted passes. But both booming headers glanced over the crossbar.

The boys dragged their bodies off the field to cheers from parents who were almost as exhausted as their players. With the score still tied, we were forced to rely on penalty kicks to determine who would advance to the Final.

The penalties began, alternating between five players on each team. Both teams hit their first three shots. I shook my head with a laugh—Mac reached all three with his fingers but was unable to redirect any away from the goal.

Ryan took our fourth and placed it in the upper right of the goal. They also hit their fourth, and tensions rose.

Calm and collected was Jack. I had named him as our fifth before the penalties began. Jack intentionally hesitated, triggering their goalkeeper to dive prematurely—which Jack then took advantage of by coolly putting the ball into the open net on the opposite side as the dejected keeper pounded his fist on the ground.

Whether he was mimicking Jack or not, the opponents' final kicker feinted to his left, but Mac didn't go for it. Clearly rattled, the player hit a weak ball straight at Mac, who was now standing tall in the goal.

Mission accomplished. On to the Final.

I checked my watch and turned to the parents. "Same field. Three o'clock. Try to relax!"

Twenty-Three

FLIPPING THE FINGER

We lost the Final 3–2. There were tears and lowered heads. As he exited the field after the final whistle, Nathan looked at me and gave a deadpan, "Shit."

I turned with him, put one arm around his shoulders, and responded in the same dire tone, "Yup. That sums it up."

As the guys quietly entered the training field later that week, Nathan asked me a rather profound question.

"Hey, Scott, before all the matches, I noticed every coach looked down at your hand while they were shaking it. Do you find that annoying?"

"Not anymore," I said.

"Why is that?" he asked.

"Confidence."

I hoped his willingness to ask such a personal question was the sign I'd been waiting for—that he'd learned to trust me. *And himself.*

In each of the following three tournaments, we won our group and advanced—twice losing in the semifinal and once in the Final (again). The focus for the next two weeks of training was building confidence in the boys. To do this, each session would pinpoint our work and include the following:

1. Dynamic stretching
2. Keep-away in groups of three to four within twenty-by-twenty-yard grids, using one ball per group
3. Eight attackers vs. eight defenders, plus a goalkeeper in pinnies on a half field
4. Stop/Start coaching points as needed

As our first session after the most recent tournament began, I called the guys in for our usual post-match evaluation. I wasn't surprised to find everyone with the same distant look as Lucas.

"You guys seem pissed. Why are you pissed?" I asked openly.

"We lost," blurted Nathan.

"Okay, so let's talk about losing," I said to open the discussion.

"Losing sucks," Alexis chirped. "Let's put that on T-shirts and sell 'em."

This broke the group into laughter, including me and Phil. We couldn't stop and had to turn away to gather ourselves.

"Are you cry-laughing, Phil?" I could barely catch my breath.

Phil turned to the group with his eyes full of tears and arms crossed, bent over, which got the entire team going.

I never asked Phil if his laughing fit was real or if it was a coaching ploy.

With no need for an evaluation, I picked up my backpack and grabbed a golf chair—which I was now using to show how I was trusting the boys—then told them to follow me to the center circle.

As I did with many of my college teams and upper-level high school teams once their play hit a certain level of quality, I simply opened the golf chair over the kickoff spot, and with our full supply of balls behind me and the portable speaker pouring out mood-setting music, sat watching play.

With "Barracuda" by Heart as the backdrop, we were off.

Whenever a learning opportunity presented itself, I'd blow my whistle to freeze play, correct the action, and set a restart—usually not allowing movement of players until the ball was played. The objective of this stop/start type of training was to allow the players to restart a move, pass, or action with the desired outcome.

A perfect training session was one where I never had to interrupt play. Since this was not expected (I'd never experienced a perfect session), one stop/start every five minutes was the target.

That weekend, I received an email from Richard Peters with the subject line "Meeting." The message was one line:

> Coach Martin,
> I want to meet you before your next training
>   session.
> Richard Peters, Director of Coaching

My response included a bit more than his ten words:

> Coach Peters,
> You must have been reading my mind... Our next
>   training session will be Thursday, as I will be
>   out of town for a few days. Does 5:30 that
>   evening work for you?
> Scott

Before we moved from Nevada, someone from the research department at Johns Hopkins University in Baltimore contacted me to ask if I was interested in helping them create a new type of myoelectric hand that would include individually moving fingers. The system I used served one function: to open and close in a pinching grip between the thumb and forefinger, plus a portion of the middle finger. But what most intrigued them was that I was bilateral—I used not one but two myoelectric hands.

To improve optics for members of Congress as more and more amputee soldiers returned from Afghanistan, the government appropriated millions of dollars to throw at the issue. But I saw a problem. With a working model set up as a computer program, the time had come for me to fly in for two days of being strapped up to the same type of receptors I used to more "simply" open and close my hands. With straps around my forearms—and accepting the failures that were sure to come by now using four fingers plus an opposing thumb—by the second day, I had mastered the program.

"The system is much more intricate than what I use," I said to one of the research assistants.

I was in familiar territory—back to when the Mad Hatter of prosthetics, Zenon Wojcik, took me down the rabbit hole to learn the more simplistic model of myoelectric hands. But if my simplistically designed hands broke down every six months and took more than two months to work their way through the tangled red tape of insurance providers to be repaired—at the cost of thousands of dollars—what was going to happen to the returning amputated veterans who would depend on these works of art?

"You'd better make them durable and cost-effective," I said rather directly while at dinner with the director of the program.

He hesitated. "Of course," he replied.

I never heard from Johns Hopkins again.

Two years later, I was given one of these hands that made it into full production and onto the arms of war veterans. True, the fingers could be moved individually. In fact, for the first time since the illness, I had an independently moving middle finger.

Within a week, the electronics fried.

There were a few people I would have liked to flip off.

I showed up at Richard Peters's office that Tuesday at 5:30 p.m., thirty minutes before training was set to begin.

"Have a seat," he started—and then continued before I got the chance to. "At all times, our coaches need to be in charge."

I nodded. "Of course."

"Our coaches should not be sitting during training," he added, having caught my eyes for the first time since I'd stood at attention in the doorway, waiting to be beckoned. His face was stern and disapproving.

My eyebrows furrowed as I tilted my head to the left. "Are you talking about the sessions where I sat on a golf chair to remove myself as the center of attention and allow the players the freedom to play unrestricted?"

His facial expression remained unchanged. "We don't sit," he retorted. He glanced at a paper on his desk.

I tried not to let my face give away that I knew nothing he said would change the way I coached. "I will assume that would not apply to a disabled person or anyone who requires an accommodation," I pushed back, graciously allowing him the opportunity to adjust his statement.

Still looking at the paper, he had only one thing to say: "Don't sit during training."

Back at practice, Phil and I had a brief check-in with the boys. When we broke for training to begin, I smirked to myself as I settled oh-so-comfortably into my golf chair and crossed my legs.

"From the top, boys! Let's strive for perfection."

Twenty-Four

SOMETIMES THERE
IS CRYING IN SOCCER

"Soccer is an emotional game—it can bite you in
the ass." —said every soccer player, ever.

I'd noticed too many teams relying on predictable tactics in their attack. Boring. I wanted the boys to add some flair to their style of play. It was time to push their creativity.

We began to designate the area behind the opponent's backline players—the enormous area of vacant grass—as the "Green." I encouraged the boys to play the ball from the midfield—and sometimes from the backs—into this space. Anytime a ball was played in the Green, they were instructed to shout, "GREEN!"

Nothing should be haphazard. Even as they played freely and creatively, every ball served had to have a purpose and be properly placed and laid into the Green. I started the boys with a drill that required teammates to position themselves twenty yards apart. Each serve had to be placed on the chest of the receiving teammate. Not an easy task, but one we did daily leading up to our final tournament. Balls went high, balls went low, balls were dodged just in time to miss some... I'll say *sensitive* areas.

Once they started to get the hang of it, I called them over.

"Now let's see if you can use what you've learned in a game," I said. The boys divided into two teams for some backyard soccer.

Owen was the first to attempt a serve to his teammate's chest. In his determination to set it up, he waited too long to pass. Jack stole the ball before Isaiah could serve it.

"Good work," I told Owen as he jogged past. "Messing up means you're learning. Keep learning."

He grinned and flashed a thumbs-up. "I'll get it next time. Or I won't."

Across the halfway line stood a coach who represented everything that was going wrong with soccer. He was decked out in full training gear, as if he were about to enter the field himself—which he basically did during the near-full training session he orchestrated just prior to the match while my kids relaxed and prepared their minds and muscles for competition. *Thanks for wasting your sprint steps before the match, buddy,* I thought.

I waited to shake his hand until the team captains met for the coin toss that would determine who possessed the ball first and who started on each half of the field. His eyes lingered on the prosthetic hand I offered. Two beats passed before he finally reached out to clasp it.

As we turned to head back to our respective sides to start our first match in group play, I caught his mouth curving into a smirk after noticing my hands. A similar expression spread across mine. *Got him,* I thought, as I returned to our bench. The poker game had begun.

As the guys finished their warm-up, I sensed that something was up with Mac. I'd put Mac in goal that day and wondered if that had something to do with it. When he jogged in for some water, I called him over.

"What's up, man?" I asked.

He shrugged.

"Something on your mind?"

He looked out at the field, where the other team was undergoing military-level drills in yet more final preparation at the command of their coach. He took a swig from his water bottle. I waited.

At last, he said, "I'm sick of being short."

I paused, surprised by his complaint. "You may be short now, but you'll grow. And if you're this good at pint-sized, you'll be even better when you're full-grown."

He sighed. "No one takes me seriously because I'm small."

I shook my head. "That's your secret weapon, then, isn't it? It's always better to be the underdog. When they take you for granted, they dig their own hole. How often do you think people see my disability and think I'm no one to worry about?"

"A lot, I guess."

"Yeah. A lot," I said. "But I use that to my advantage. Like with that coach over there. What do you think of him?"

Mac wrinkled his nose. "He's arrogant."

"Exactly. He thinks he's hot stuff. So I made sure he saw my disability before the match started. He'll think a team led by a disabled person couldn't possibly compete with his."

Mac narrowed his eyes. "Yeah, right. We'll show him."

"You bet we will."

True to Mac's and my words, within the first ten minutes of the game, we'd pestered the opposing team for a 2–0 lead. It set the coach in a frenzy, and he took his anger out on his players in a verbal tirade. In the second half, post-tirade, his boys scored a goal. It didn't concern Phil or me, but sensing that our kids needed a pause, Phil shouted, "What's the score, boys?"

Everyone yelled back, "Zero–zero!"

This prompted the opposing coach to point out three of his players by name. "Move your ass, Jacob, Michael, and Josh," he hollered at them in disappointment.

After we won the match 4–1, I had had enough from this bully in athletic wear. In our final handshake, I applied unusual pressure and looked him square in the eyes.

"Don't abuse the game," I warned.

He looked at me blankly, then scoffed and turned back toward his team.

In my view, coaching was done during training. My role during match play was simple:

1. Recognize the patterns of the opponent
2. Adjust to these patterns and force the opponent out of their comfort zone
3. Note topics for the next training sessions

Of course, there were learning opportunities, positive comments, and fist bumps during play—but no negatives.

After winning our group and heading into our first match of the tournament playoffs, Mac controlled the goal. Jack continued to run the back line, and Liam the midfield. For the first ten minutes, no one from either team scored—until Nathan.

Liam had the ball but was under pressure from the other team. He chipped it with his right foot, sending it in a long arch. It sailed thirty yards overhead, right into Nathan's path.

Nathan didn't miss a beat. He slid the ball to the left of the goalkeeper as if he had been doing it his whole life. It was a beautiful play—one reminiscent of a pass from Joe Montana to Jerry Rice during the glory years of the San Francisco 49ers.

Nathan whooped out loud and threw both fists in the air. When he glanced in my direction, I did the same—at least as best I could.

He scored three more goals in the match, establishing himself as the top goal scorer I knew he was. They'd just earned their spot in yet another Final.

As Nathan jogged off the field, I clapped him on the back. "Do me a favor and go easy on the next team," I told him. "My arm's getting sore from all the fist-pumping."

Nathan grinned. "Not a chance."

Jerry Stark also opened me up to coaching, soccer administration, and teaching. After he left the program to start one of the first select-level clubs in our area of the state, Oshkosh United, he recommended me to be player-coach my junior year. After meeting with Roger, the head of the Recreation Department, I told him I only wanted to play varsity teams within the region, with the objective of receiving varsity status for what I hoped would be the senior season for our main core of players.

With wins over NCAA Division I, II, and III programs (though not within the window I had hoped), we went 25–7–2 over two seasons. Nonetheless, as we exited the field after a win in the final home match of my college career, the university chancellor flashed me a thumbs-up. With that endorsement, we gave the gift of varsity status to the players who followed.

After the win, the college newspaper printed a photo of me puffing a cigar and holding a bottle of Yoo-hoo while wearing a T-shirt from our opponent. I was honored to be invited to interview for the head coaching position, but I wasn't surprised when the university tabbed Toby Bares for the job. Bares had experience at the college level with a varsity program. Heck, I had yet to even graduate. I had a lot to learn.

Soccer players tend to be visual learners. So before each match, I used blue discs to lay out our formation. For the entire summer, I had set down a design that utilized either five or six midfielders in varying patterns. But as the boys gathered around for the system of this match, I held back one disc. The boys looked at the 3–4–2 formation displayed on the grass.

"Hey, Scott, you forgot one," Liam said.

"Nope," I replied. "We're playing ten versus ten this match."

That got me some strange looks.

I pointed the blue disc I was still holding at Luke. A skinny kid with a hefty sweep of brown hair to his left, Luke had shown some of the best defensive skills on the team.

"You're going to deny number seven the ball. Don't let him *breathe*. Make them play with ten players," I instructed.

Luke smiled and nodded. "He's mine."

"Release the Kraken!" I proclaimed.

Luke proceeded to frustrate the tall blond so much that, for the first time, his coiffed hairdo—with the same lime-green headband as their uniform color—began to sag, weighed down by his sweaty locks. As we neared the end of the match, the score remained tied at 0–0—until Luke clipped Golden Boy's heels thirty yards from our goal. It was a legitimate foul, resulting in a direct free kick.

With two minutes to go, number seven stepped up for his first clear shot at our goal—and his opportunity to breathe.

No sound came from the crowd that surrounded the field. Number seven took four steps back from the ball. He sized up Mac, who was standing with his weight balanced and knees loose in the goal. He approached the ball and took a shot. The ball arced high into the air. Mac leapt for it, hands outstretched. But he was a foot too low. The ball sailed between his gloves and the crossbar and into the goal.

Seventeen heads dropped. Luke fell to his knees as Phil and I exchanged sullen looks.

The boys gave it their all in the remaining time, but we couldn't make up for the one goal against us.

The final whistle signaled us as another tournament bridesmaid.

There were no words of encouragement I could give—or wanted to give. I didn't want to lie to them. This loss hurt.

The opposing coach approached Luke as the players left the field. "You're the best defender I've seen all summer," he told him, shaking the boy's hand.

Luke thanked him, grief still clouding his bright blue eyes.

Twenty-Five

MINNESOTA FATS

After the last game of the tournament, with two weeks until training for state league play ahead of me, I took off my sweaty sock to find that the ulceration on my right foot had returned. It taunted me like Randy Quaid in *Independence Day*: "Hello, boys, I'm *ba-aaaack!*"

Fuck me.

Somehow, I was able to secure an evaluation with a wound specialist at the University of Washington Medical Center in Seattle the next afternoon.

"You have a problem," said the wound specialist.

Yeah, no shit, Sherlock, I thought.

He made a call to another department, then directed me to another building to be seen by another professional. But as I crossed the sky bridge, I noticed I was heading toward the surgery pavilion.

I was confused. I approached a volunteer sitting at the information desk. "Is this correct?"

She looked up at me. "Yes, you're in the right place."

"I'll cut along here," the doctor explained as he ran his finger across my shin, a few inches below my knee.

"A BK?!" I blurted. "You think the solution is to take *another* part of me?" I added pointedly.

I don't know if he even responded. I had already tuned him out.

"That's not happening," I assured him as I popped off the exam table and left.

The school year was about to begin, as was training for the upcoming state league season. But first, we needed to hold our individual player evaluations for the summer season. At the same picnic table where I'd first met my team of soccer rats and their families three months earlier, I sat with each player and their parents over a two-day period. I came ready with a formal evaluation that included a rating for each boy on a scale from one to five in the areas of technical ability, tactical awareness, physical fitness, and emotional maturity.

I ended each and every meeting with two questions:

"How do you feel about going all summer without winning a championship?"

They all responded similarly: "It hurts bad."

Then, "And what about the final match?"

Again, similar responses—and even some tears: "That's not happening again," was the frustrated gist from each and every player.

Their answers told me two things: first, they were no longer little kids—they were mad and had matured. Second, they were ready for the state league season to begin.

The parents dropped off the guys at an area bowling complex that offered snacks, drinks, and three pool tables.

"But, Scott, how are you going to shoot pool without real hands?" Ryan asked.

"Truthfully, right now, I have no idea. I'm going to sit back and evaluate your movements and then come up with a solution," I responded. "Does that process sound familiar?"

"Yeah," Mac said as he confidently chalked his cue stick like he'd done it a thousand times before. "Like when we observe our opponents before a match."

"Wow, Mac—or should I call you Minnesota Fats? Have you played pool before?" I asked, referencing the legendary pool shark who I wasn't sure he knew.

"I'm not fat. And yes, I have. Eight ball, anyone?" the pint-sized hustler spouted, breaking the ice for all of us.

All seventeen players showed up, so to divide everyone into pairs, I told them to line up according to birthday. Phil couldn't show, so when I found a gap where I belonged, I jumped into line.

A chorus of "Oooohs" erupted when they noticed that I'd included myself in the competition.

"Now we'll have an even number of nine teams. With four players playing on three tables, how many of us will be waiting to play?"

"Six players, or three teams, will not be playing," Jack calculated.

"For a center back, you definitely should be able to evaluate and quickly solve a problem," I added. "Now—winner stays!"

After I paired the boys up and set opponents at each table, I grabbed a stool by the bar and poured myself a Mountain Dew from a pitcher. A minute later, Isaac approached me.

"So, teammate," Isaac said, tilting his head forward and peering into my eyes. "I see two problems you need to solve."

He'd clearly evaluated my situation in detail. "What's your solution to your problem of how to hold and use the cue?"

"That one's easy," I said confidently. "I'll hold the base as I used to."

"And as for where the shooting end will rest...?" Isaac cocked an eyebrow, having seemingly cornered me with this one.

I showed Isaac my left hand, which was open. "Imagine my hand as normal. Here's the metacarpal," I said, running my right myo-thumb along the third bone from the distal end.

"This knuckle is the carpometacarpal joint," I continued, pointing to the knuckle nearest the wrist. "And this," I pointed to the next knuckle, "is the interphalangeal joint."

Isaac watched my hand intently as I demonstrated my tactic. "I'm going to rest the cue between these two knuckles," I said, concluding my anatomy lecture.

Isaac wasn't convinced. "But that area's wide—it's gonna be tough to keep the cue in line."

"That's the best I've got, buddy," I responded. "That's my best game plan."

Isaac and I finished even. Mac and his teammate Alexis only left their table to eat their burgers.

Following our first ouster from play, Isaac unloaded another question on me—a more intimate one this time.

"Since you became disabled, have you ever experienced discrimination?"

With a blue plastic tumbler of green Dew in my left hand, making for an interesting color combination, I sat back on my stool with my eyebrows raised, considering the gravity of the question. It seemed that Isaac and I had something in common.

"Yes, I have. And it angers me," I said after a pause.

"But that only happens after the offending person knows about my history—or after he—always *he*—notices my hands." We'd cut right to the nitty-gritty.

"Can you give me an example?" Isaac asked intently.

"I can give you two," I said. I went on to tell Isaac about the college athletic director who asked his secretary why he had interviewed a man with no hands—how I overheard his snide remark and how it had made me feel awful, inferior, small.

"The other was before an interview. Another athletic director called me to arrange for a meeting and told me that he 'loved my credentials' and looked forward to getting together." I paused and sighed.

"When he entered the waiting area outside his office, he was all smiles. And then he reached out his hand to shake mine. Immediately, his eyes shot to my hand, and he pulled back. He rushed the whole interview, barely asking me anything. He even told me to respond quickly because there was another candidate coming in immediately after me.

A few days later, he called and said they were going in a 'different direction.'"

I'd fallen from the open doors that came with being a white man to the latched doors that came with a visible disability.

I decided to shift the focus. "Being Black in America, I can only imagine what your experience has been."

With raised brows, we looked at each other and shrugged our shoulders.

Then a table opened.

My brief conversation with Isaac took me back to a moment with my Ethiopian son. One afternoon, after I picked him up from kindergarten, he climbed into the car, turned to me, and asked, "When am I going to turn white?"

In that instant, I realized how far we still hadn't come in America.

Twenty-Six

ARE THE CAPTIONS ON?

The boys approached the training field in small groups to begin preparations for state league play. This was when the real competition would begin. Starting with their next match, every win and loss would be tallied to determine the ultimate league champion.

We'd play every team in the league twice—in home and away games. Three points for a win, one point for a tie. Whoever earned the most points by the end of the season was the champion. Everything we'd done so far, from training to the summer tournaments, had been preparing the boys for league competition.

As the guys dribbled their soccer balls onto the field, I was struck by how much they'd changed since our first meeting. There was a swagger to them now. They walked with their shoulders high and relaxed, chins up. They stepped onto the field as if they knew they belonged. More than that, they stepped onto the field as if they *owned* it. In many ways, my efforts to build their confidence had been completed.

Phil must have been thinking along similar lines, because he gave a small laugh and commented on how many of the boys had let their hair grow since our first meeting. "I doubt many of them have been close to a pair of scissors in three months."

My soccer rats had grown into their name.

"Cool," I replied. "Very cool."

After our loss in the last tournament's Final, I knew what this training session needed: one of the best albums ever produced—and the one that represented my feeling for the game above all others—R. L. Burnside's *Come On In.*

"Lace 'em up, gentlemen," I said. "We're playing backyard soccer today. Turn off your brains and let's roll."

There was no longer any hesitation when I let them loose for some old-school soccer. Their play was as free-flowing as their new long-haired style. I felt a surge of pride at who they had become—and were still becoming.

After the warm-up game, Phil and I had the guys bring a portable full-sized goal to the top of the penalty box. We told them to break into teams of two to play competitive games of two versus two within the penalty box using two goals—no goalkeepers. The first team to score would stay on, and a new pair would enter immediately to keep up the pressure. The objective was to stay on the field by scoring.

As I watched Mac and Lucas battle it out against Nate and Stroh, a familiar stocky shadow appeared beside me. It was the first time in over a month that Richard Peters had graced us with his presence. I would have been glad if it were the last.

"League play starts next week," he said.

"We'll be ready," I replied.

"What formation will you be playing?" he asked. "I prefer four backs at this level."

Before I could respond, Jack walked up to us and chimed in.

"Our formation changes during play and is based on winning the midfield to begin our counterattacks as high as possible and to keep our opponents facing their own goal as often as possible. We use a lot of mathematics to keep the odds in our favor—like counting cards when playing blackjack."

I was blown away and could only flash a Cheshire Cat smile at my young scholar. Richard, on the other hand, said nothing and donned his usual stern, unchanging expression.

Jack turned to me and winked.

Richard turned and headed to the next field.

After he was at a safe distance, Jack and I fist-bumped. I turned up the volume on R. L.'s "It's Bad You Know."

Our first league match was at high noon, two hours south of Bellingham in a Seattle suburb. The soccer complex was an expanse of open fields rimmed by trees. In the distance, the snow-capped top of Mount Rainier extended up toward the cloudless sky.

The guys were relaxed, despite it being their first league match. As they each began their warm-up routine, I conducted my own pregame analysis of our opponent. Jack came to stand beside me at midfield. He hadn't yet changed into his kit and was sporting a USA Alexi Lalas jersey.

"There you go," I said. "Alexi Lalas. That's you!" All he needed was the long beard, and he'd be the spitting image of the redheaded former U.S. Men's National Team player.

Jack shook his head to swish around his long orange locks. We laughed and turned back to the field in front of us.

"What do you see?" I asked him.

Jack squinted and cocked his head. "They're technically decent, but rely too much on their right foot," he assessed. "Decent speed. Number ten looks to be their best player. I guess he'll probably play as their central attacker."

And he was right on every count.

During the match, my soccer rats were successful in their attack but not in their scoring. They repeatedly shot directly into the goalkeeper's open arms. It was almost as if they no longer believed in their ability to win. The loss in the last tournament may have hit them harder than I'd realized.

At halftime, they ambled slowly from the field, heads hanging low—until I reminded them that we *always* jogged off the field. They picked up the pace. When they had all gathered around, I prepared to begin my mid-match analysis—but Jack beat me to the punch.

"Dudes, we need to stop thinking," he said, adjusting the black spaghetti headband he'd taken to wearing across his forehead to keep his hair out of his eyes. Alexi Lalas, indeed.

"I couldn't put it any better," I said. "Do I need to add anything?"

No one replied. It was the shortest halftime spiel of my entire coaching career.

Their second half was masterful. The frustration was gone. We managed to score, and Nate, our goalkeeper for the day, kept the ball out of our net. It seemed that the cloud of their loss in the tournament Final had vanished. With fewer than thirty seconds on the clock, it looked like we'd take the match 1–0.

Then our opponent's number ten stole the ball. A long-legged kid, he gunned it for our goal. Nate flicked the ball over the crossbar, awarding them a corner kick, but collided with an opposing player in the process. As the two boys fell to the ground, the ref threw his hands up, one over the other, to signal a stop of the clock.

As Nate got to his feet, I glanced at my watch. Four seconds remained.

Four seconds.

"I don't like this," I said nervously to Phil as I pressed pause on the countdown timer on my watch. Had play continued, we would have won. But as today's overprotection of players goes, the referee stopped everything to check on Nate.

In my decades as a coach, player, and spectator, I'd never seen a team in the lead with only a few seconds to go suffer from a player going down.

This was a first.

The ref waited to restart the clock until the opponents set for their corner kick. As number ten served the ball, I resumed the timer on my watch.

Four. The ball arced upward at an angle toward our goal.

Three. Their tallest player jumped into the air.

Two. He arched back.

One. The ball careened off his head, straight for our goal.

Zero. The crack of the ball hitting the back of the net reverberated across the field.

The ref blew his whistle. My boys dropped to their knees, heads in their hands.

I had no words. I could only shrug my shoulders and shake my head.

On my drive back to Bellingham, an idea struck me: *brownies.* Following a tough loss with my earlier teams, I'd made brownies —moist, chocolatey goodness that no one can ignore. This was definitely a good time for brownies.

When the team gathered for our next training session, I presented a large pan of ooey-gooey decadence. They just about drooled.

"Hey, Scott, one's missing," Lucas noticed.

I shrugged like I didn't know what he was talking about, then licked my lips and winked.

League standings were posted online after each weekend match. Following our fifth match, we were tied for second with one other team at thirteen points. We were two points behind a familiar opponent: the lime-green team from Seattle that had beaten us in the last tournament Final. After match number eight, we were still behind the "Limees," as I'd tabbed them, who remained without a loss or tie.

"Here we go!" I announced with enthusiasm as we began training for the big matchup.

Isaac, who had really come into his own over the last few weeks, called out, "Are we ready to do this, boys?"

Playing our lime-green opponents again meant that we needed to tweak our game plan this time around. "Yes, Luke will mark Goldilocks again," I said, just as he had last time.

This stirred the boys into rowdy chants of "Kraken! Kraken! Kraken!" in support of Luke's play.

"Okay, okay, shut up," I said with a smile, holding my open left hand up to my lips. "But here's the change: Have any of you watched at least the first two *Rocky* movies?"

To my surprise, almost every hand went up. "Wow. Okay, great. So, in their first fight, Rocky went full southpaw on Apollo Creed—with his left hand, right? What change did Mickey make for the second fight?"

"Rocky used his right more often!" Nick blurted.

"Correct," I responded.

Luke piped up. "So we're *not* going with the man mark?"

"Yes and no." My response created some murmurs of confusion.

"Luke will neutralize number seven until the final twenty minutes. Then we'll switch to an umbrella of four backs, four midfielders, and one attacker in front of Jack. At that time, delay play to absorb every single tick of the clock." Nods from the crowd.

I added, "Of course, I'm expecting a lead by that time." More nodding from the crowd.

"This takes us to the emphasis of our training for the week." I placed my portable coaching board on the golf chair and diagrammed the corner kick play we had practiced during our most recent sessions.

After our final session for the week, Matt Stroh approached me and offered to carry my golf chair.

"Hey, Scott?"

"What's up, Strohmeister?"

"Today, I gave a speech during English about what I've noticed about people with disabilities since we've been working together."

I nodded, impressed. "Very cool. What's your take?"

He explained, "I opened by asking the class what world group includes nearly two billion people and pumps thirteen trillion dollars into the world economies."

We stopped, and I paused, interested in the rest of the opening.

"No one had an answer," Matt said. "I then asked if any of them had a person with a disability in their family."

"Did any hands go up?" I asked.

"There was some hesitation, but some hands did go up." He looked up at me.

"I asked my teacher if I could speak with you and then continue my speech on Monday." He added, "Give me an example of how you've experienced being treated unfairly by someone who doesn't have a disability."

As we loaded the gear into my car, I allowed myself a moment to come up with a response that was both candid and useful.

"Hit your classmates—and your teacher—with this question: Is it common for your teachers to turn the closed captions on when playing a video for the class?"

Matt paused in thought, taking his own moment to digest my query. Then he lit up.

"Because there may be students who need captions but don't ask because asking will draw attention to their disability."

I smiled proudly. "Way to go, Stroh."

Twenty-Seven

THE OLD SWITCHEROO

It's been so long since the illness that I rarely look back at the division between pre-illness and post-illness life. Of course, I *wonder*—if I hadn't become sick—how things would be different. There were a million possibilities, of course. Would UW–Eau Claire have won a national championship? If they did, how many titles? At what level would I be coaching five, ten, twenty years after that? And where? What turns would my life have taken? Would it have been better than the life I have?

We were still two damn points behind the Limees—but we were on the road, and I was loving our position. As was my norm before a match, I strolled to the center of the field and took in all the free information the opposing coach had to give. And just as they did during the tournament Final, they were running drills. I turned around to my guys. Mac had asked Nathan to take shots on him in goal; our midfielders were playing rondo (a form of keep-away); the backs were lobbing forty-yard balls to each other;

and Jack was bouncing his head to music blasting through his earbuds. I sighed in satisfaction. *Exactly the way I like it.*

After the officials checked our player cards, player cleats, shin guards, and jewelry removal, I asked them to gather.

"I'm ready. Are you guys ready?" I casually asked.

The boys all gave various forms of "no" in response. I raised my brow.

"*Got ya!*" they responded in unison.

I rolled my eyes and smiled. "Well done, morons. Very well done."

Neither team got a quality shot on goal during the first half. Luke shut down number seven, who never even sniffed the ball. Play occurred between the two penalty boxes for the full forty minutes.

During the half, I met with Isaac, Stroh, Nathan, and Liam— the four potential pieces to the winning goal.

Ten minutes into the second half, we finally received a corner kick—this one from the left, Isaac's side. Understanding his role, Isaac set the ball on the outer edge of the corner arc. Five players, including Nathan, formed an hourglass at the top of the penalty box in line with the far post. I'd been successfully using this play since my early coaching days, and our opponent had seen us run it a few times during our first match against each other. But this time, we added a wrinkle.

Rather than Nathan—our tallest player with a good heading technique—attacking the middle just outside the six-yard box and the middle of the goal, he looped around to a spot outside the far post and farther from the goal. Isaac laid his serve farther than normal to Nathan, who was unmarked.

All the opposing players, including the goalkeeper, who had been expecting the ball to come to the center, now scurried to Nathan. This cleared the near side of the goal. As the play was designed, Nathan headed the ball over the shifting mob of lime green to the now wide-open Liam, who casually nodded the ball across the end line for the opening goal.

I didn't intervene in their well-deserved celebration. They had certainly earned it. Now, we needed to manage the clock for thirty excruciating minutes. But the guys knew the game plan and took their time retrieving every ball out of bounds, every goal kick, every offensive free kick, and every minor injury. We were absolutely milking it.

Finally, with twenty minutes left, I gave the word. "SHIFT!"

Luke pried himself off number seven and moved into a defensive umbrella in front of Jack. The expectation was for Jack to play without having to mark an opponent and just clean up anything that might get past our back line. As the clock dipped inside of ten minutes, anything that came to our backs was cleared up the field as far as possible.

Tick tock, I thought.

The whistle finally blew. We won, taking the coveted three points. My young players had learned how to truly win a match.

The lights over the field flickered on as our training session neared its end. It was shaping up to be a perfect evening—until, of course, *Mr. Inopportune* showed up.

"How's the season going?" Richard asked as he walked up to me.

I didn't turn to look at him. *Why give him the respect he refused to give me?* But that's not my style, so I turned. "Undefeated and a point up heading into the second half of play."

"Good. Be careful not to push them too hard," he said. "They're only C-level players."

I ignored him. Again, criticizing my young players for no reason.

He continued. "They might not be able to handle the pressure."

I clenched my jaw. *Don't say anything,* I thought. *Don't take the bait.* But I did. I had to defend my boys.

"These kids have won, tied, and lost matches. They've made up ground after falling behind and lost ground after being ahead.

They understand winning, and they understand losing. They can handle anything that's thrown at them."

I stood and waited for a response, but none came. He didn't even look at me. He put his hands in the pockets of his sweatpants and walked to the next field.

I fished a stick of Wrigley's out of my backpack, then noticed all the players and Phil watching me. I grinned at them. Phil gave me a thumbs-up.

Before moving to Washington, I was asked by the head of the amputee clinic at a Veterans Administration hospital outside Las Vegas to visit and discuss their push to be designated as a Poly-trauma & Amputation Network Site (PANS). With so many veterans returning from war missing limbs, it seemed like a no-brainer for both of us.

"I want you to work with us, Scott," he said after our discussion, comparing my background and his needs.

"Of course," I responded.

"You would be a great benefit to our amputees as they adjust to their new normal."

But there was a hang-up: money. *Federal* money.

For months, I was copied on all emails to and from the administrators who held the purse strings. The final message from the highest person on the VA totem pole opened without a salutation and included only two dry sentences. The first was all it took:

At the present time, we do not have any plans to increase the number of PANS-designated facilities, so I am not sure exactly what the process for this will look like in the future.

It should be no wonder why I have disdain for those who fail to recognize the disability community or disabled individuals. Everyone deserves respect—at least initially.

Three weeks after moving into first place, we settled for a tie. With the Limees back on a winning streak, they had moved ahead of us in the standings.

Our next match was at Civic Stadium in Bellingham, a massive athletic complex with everything from sports fields to a dirt bike park. More importantly, it was the home field for all three high schools in Bellingham and, as such, would become the home field for this group in a few years.

Constantly watching the weekly standings was tough on the guys, and it was tough on me. In my mind, I'd been juggling training, match preparation, match management, and the emotions of a group of young men who had been told they weren't good enough. I needed a distraction—something to relax everyone. And I had one more rabbit to pull from my coaching bag of tricks.

For our final training session before playing the fourth-place team in our league, the guys arrived to find four discs on the ground in the shape of a diamond, each thirty yards apart. One ball rested in the middle, and one portable goal was behind what by now was viewed as home plate of a baseball field.

After the players lined up, teams were set by calling off numbers one and two.

"Here's the game, guys," I announced before explaining the contest.

"It's closer to kickball than to baseball. No hands—play it the same as soccer. The object is to not be caught off base when the ball enters the goal."

As the simple rules sank into their skulls, I added, "Everyone is up once per inning."

"So, your final batter should be the person with the greatest chance for a home run because he ends the inning," Ryan injected, as I nodded.

From my youngest team of soccer rats to my college teams, I'd closed out every season with this game. Part of good coaching is not being afraid to change things up. Sensing the need for a tweak to our training, the timing was right to move the kickball game forward.

"Give me one player from each team. Rock, paper, scissors—winner chooses to field or kick first."

Every team, every year, I witnessed the same results: big smiles on the faces of the players.

It was match day. Like every match, this one was important. We remained undefeated but still behind first. I popped a piece of Wrigley's in my mouth as Liam stepped up to take our kickoff. He tapped it to Nathan, and the match was on.

At halftime, we were up five–zero, and our opponent had yet to cross into our half of the field with the ball under control.

"You know, guys," I said as the boys settled in during halftime, "with another half like that, you'll pull off a perfect game.

"Winning without giving up a shot is one thing—but to deny your opponent from entering your side of the field with the ball under control is a perfect game."

"They have crossed the halfway line," Nathan stated.

"But not with the ball under control!" Jugraj spouted.

"Jack, you and I are so bored we could play cards in defense," Mac added, stirring chuckles and shaking heads.

"I'm serious, guys. Let's go for a perfect game," Jugraj said with conviction—this time to the nodding heads of a committed team. "They don't enter our half!"

Though the score was reported as 8–0, the boys experienced the feeling of completing a perfect game.

I never told them I had made up there being such a thing as a perfect game in soccer.

Twenty-Eight

IF THE SOCCER CLEAT FITS

> Hi folks,
>
> After 17 matches, we sit in second place at 47 points with a record of 15 wins, 0 losses, and 2 ties. The Limees lead with 48 points at 16–1–0.
>
> The day before the match against the Limees, I emailed this to the parents and players, along with a quote from John Wooden:
>
> "Winning is like a reputation. Your reputation is what you're perceived to be; your character is what you really are."
>
> –Scott

J ose was away on Wednesday, so we were going with three team-only training sessions that final week. I told the guys we'd substitute the scrimmage with a two-versus-two tournament since we had a player away.

As the guys arrived at the Tuesday session, I turned to Phil. "Do you notice something different about the boys?"

He paused for a moment. "Calmness. And a swagger."

With my coaching board propped up on the golf chair, I'd placed the magnets in a new design before calling the guys over.

"What do you notice about this system?" I started.

Jack pointed out that he'd be playing with the same umbrella backline we used later in the last match against the Limees.

"So, no man-mark?" Luke asked.

I nodded. "No man-mark. What else do you see?" I prodded. I was looking for them to notice something so obvious that they might have thought it was an error.

Nathan caught it. "There are two attackers, but they're not symmetrical ... one's on the far right, and one's in the center."

"Nice catch, Nathan," I confirmed. "What's the purpose of leaving the left bare?"

I heard a few mumbles but no clear answers.

"Think back to our two matches against them. How many backs did they use?"

"Three," Jack answered.

I added a second factor. "How did those three backs respond every time we attacked down a flank?"

Isaac jumped excitedly into the fray, unafraid of responding incorrectly. His confidence had really grown. "They left the weak side open."

"Give that man a Kewpie doll!" I exclaimed with a whisk of my hand. "So, what do you suppose they'll do if we only play with a central attacker plus a right wing? Or a central attacker plus a left wing?" I asked, watching seventeen light bulbs turn on in seventeen brains.

Half a dozen players all proclaimed the same response in various ways.

"You have two sessions to learn yet another new system," I instructed, walking toward center field. They trailed behind me, determinedly exclaiming:

"We've got this!"

"Yeah—always leave your opponent guessing."
"And force them to adjust to us."
"And if they don't..."
"BOOM!"

All season long, the ulcer on the bottom of my foot never progressed. But it was always on my mind. Though very slowly, it had healed a bit after my prosthetist adjusted the footbed of my right brace. But I knew I was still in danger of infection, and I needed to find a more knowledgeable professional.

"Did you bring your thinking cap?" I said as my new prosthetist, Thomas, entered the room for my appointment.

Tom was part of a prosthetics group with offices along the Puget Sound. They offered a carbon-fiber brace that unloaded pressure from areas of the foot prone to breakdown.

"Sure, we can solve your problem," Tom said after looking over my foot.

"Well, Tom," I sighed, "that makes me happy as a clam at high tide."

After a pause to think about my shellfish analogy, he asked, "Can you stay long enough so I can cast your lower legs and feet?"

"Hell yes," came out of my mouth faster than I could even process it.

Two weeks later, Tom left me a message on my cell phone. "Scott, can you stop by the office at eight o'clock tomorrow morning to pick up your new braces?"

Kickoff for the championship—our final match of the season—was at 1:00 p.m. on the main field of our home complex. Richard Peters emailed me that he wanted to meet in his office at noon. He always knew how to put a dent in my day.

"Come on in," Richard said. "Big match today."

I sat down across from him. "The guys are ready."

He looked at me—for once. "I want to talk to you about handling an important match like this."

I tried to keep a straight face. *What the hell?* I thought. *Did he ever read my résumé?*

"Your boys need to be prepared to play at their best—play relaxed," he added.

I tilted my head, wondering if he was actually being serious or was about to break from the bit and tell me that he knew I had this in the bag. I thought about Charlie Sheen in *Eight Men Out*: "I may be dumb, fellas, but I ain't stupid." I bit my tongue.

Our meeting ended with Richard Peters glancing up and saying, "Good luck." Something told me he wouldn't appreciate the tuxedo T-shirt I had concealed under my coaching jacket, just in case I needed to lighten the mood at some point before or during the match.

I knew I didn't need to be hovering over my guys before the game. Instead, I focused on the opposition, trying to get a read on the nuances of their play as they warmed up. But while watching the Limees take practice shots on goal, I noticed something different. I scanned the field to double-check what I thought I was seeing.

"What the hell?" I said under my breath. "Number seven is in goal."

I called Jack over. "Can you spot number seven—the kid with the golden locks—on the field? Or in the stands?"

He turned to me, wide-eyed, with the same conclusion. "He's playing goalkeeper."

"Call the boys in," I requested. "Let's talk."

I silently pondered our options as my players jogged toward me. *Change? Or go with the left-handed or right-handed approach?*

When they had gathered, I made the announcement. "Our buddy number seven seems to be playing goalkeeper today."

Heads turned toward their goal.

"We're sticking with our plan," I said, standing behind the coaching board displaying our purposely lopsided formation.

"They're one point ahead of us in the standings, so all they need is a tie for the title," I said, scanning the group.

"They don't need to score ... *unless we score.*"

Heads nodded with affirmative conviction.

Our opponents howled a chant, ready to charge into battle. It was about to begin. I unzipped my jacket to display the tuxedo T-shirt. "This is a big match, gentlemen. So, I dressed up for the occasion." It took but a moment for all the boys to burst out in laughter. Mission accomplished.

I yelled among the roaring laughter, "You got this?!"

The referee blew his whistle from the center circle, beckoning our starting eleven to take the field.

Mac shouted a final, "Let's kick some ass, boys!"

It was match time.

Growing up regularly attending church, I once asked our young assistant pastor where God came from. With a smile, he told me he had often pondered the same question, then said, "Don't get too deep into it or your brain will explode."

Dreams can leave us feeling similarly discombobulated. For years after first leaving the hospital, I had countless versions of the same dream. I was always running on air, bounding from space to space like Tarzan's chimpanzee sidekick, Cheeta, scampering from branch to branch. Dreams like these stayed with me for years.

I'd run all day now if I could.

As expected, the Limees opened the match in a formation obviously meant to control the midfield, with three backs, five midfielders, and two forwards in the middle. Their three largest players made for a startling group across their back line, but they didn't seem comfortable. They were way too focused on that stupid little round thing rolling between people's feet.

Starting with our two forwards playing "right-handed"—Nathan slightly right of center and Stroh pulled wide—all our movement from the defense and midfield loaded the right. Patiently, Isaac held his position on the left side of the midfield without venturing too far forward.

Because of our shift—and the shift of their backs to our right—Stroh had trouble getting behind their backs from the right wing. As each minute on the clock ticked away, the Limees got excited. My boys were unfazed.

I overheard Owen and Nick on the bench.

"They think that we can't get the ball into their scoring zone," the first said.

The other noted, "Yeah, but look how far their right back is shifting toward the center—he's leaving a lot of green unmarked."

Suddenly, Stroh nutmegged (played the ball between the legs of the opponent) the last defender between him and the goal. Panic struck their center and right backs, and they both charged Stroh, leaving plenty of green for Isaac to slide into on the left front. The Limee goalkeeper moved tight against the goalpost, readying himself for the onslaught, but it was no matter. Stroh laid a perfectly weighted diagonal pass to an oncoming Isaac, who dribbled the ball into an open goal.

"YES! YES! YES!" I yelled. I didn't care if people thought I was crazy—these were my boys, and they were making me very proud.

I sat down in my trusty golf chair and observed the wild chants of our players. From the far sideline, their families were doing the same.

Thirty minutes later, the half ended with us up 1–0. The players on the bench greeted sweaty backs and palms with way-to-go pats and high fives. As always, the first minutes were for the boys to rest and rehydrate.

Then we got to strategizing. "When will number seven move onto the field?" I asked. "When—not if—he moves from the goal onto the field, I'll call for someone to move into the umbrella for Luke, who becomes golden boy's shadow, and we play ten versus ten. Got it?"

The guys nodded.

We need a win, not a tie, I thought, instead of saying it out loud. I wanted to avoid placing any more pressure on them than they already felt.

"If he stays in goal to start the second half, we stay right-handed for the first ten minutes, then switch to our left," I continued.

Liam took the bait. "Just like Rocky, but we're changing from right to left." I smiled.

To my surprise, golden boy started the second half in their goal. With that, we continued to overload the right, though not as effectively—they had switched their outside backs, providing more speed and better coverage of Isaac, who was now on our right side. As we did in the first half, our midfielders forced the ball toward a sideline, which limited space and became an additional defender. The boys did a remarkable job of turning the line into their teammate.

With no clear options in the middle of the field, our opponent was pinned. With the additional pressure the sideline placed on their attack, Jack could play freely from his center-back position—like a boa constrictor, choking off fruitless attacks.

Ten minutes into the second half, I called out, "ROCKY!" and the guys shifted to a left-handed attack. Just as they did before our first goal, all the Limees shifted toward the ball, leaving the right side exposed—a lovely stretch of green for Isaac to run into from his withdrawn midfield position. In the blink of an eye, he slapped in our second goal off a nifty pass by Stroh from the left flank.

The boys and the stands went wild—but I was still holding

my breath. There was still plenty of time on the clock. All they needed to do was tie to rip the championship from our grasp.

As expected, Goldilocks was pulled from the goal. During the next stoppage in play, he quickly changed to his lime-green field jersey, number seven, and reentered the match.

And as expected, our players prepared for Luke to go full Kraken on the new forward. As the scoreboard clock moved inside twenty minutes, I shouted out, "TICK! TOCK!" It was just as much for me as it was for them. I knew the boys could milk the clock.

At fifteen minutes to go, the Limees were awarded a corner kick, but the ball bent behind our goal. I could tell the pressure of the clock was building on them.

Tick. Tock.

With ten minutes to go, Jack directed our backs forward and into their end of the field as we built a quality attack. Nathan pinged a shot off the left post.

Tick. Tock.

"Nice push, Jack!" I yelled to our defensive commander. Jack smiled and gave me a thumbs-up.

It was getting near time to start sending everything long. We had to make every second that ticked by add more and more pressure on the Limees.

Now inside five minutes, Mac tipped a wicked shot from thirty yards over our goal, then wiggled his index finger as a warning that nothing was getting past him. Phil and I looked at each other and started laughing.

Tick. Tock.

With ten seconds to go, Luke stripped the ball from number seven and cleared it into the deepest corner of their side of the field.

Tick. Tock.

There was no need to retrieve the ball. The final whistle blew. Phil and I hugged and watched everyone swarm Mac. It seemed the soccer cleat fit this Cinderella.

An undefeated state league title. Not bad for a mangy group of kids that no one thought would amount to much. True soccer rats.

Twenty-Nine

THE JOY OF MY LIFE

It's been a month since our final match. The season culminated in the boys receiving medals at the club's end-of-year event. Always a big fanfare, this year included over one thousand players and their families.

We filled the seats beneath the gilded dome of Mount Baker Theater as each team took their turn onstage. Coaches made their usual speeches about their teams' accomplishments or told hard-luck stories while players were handed ribbons or had their necks draped in medals. When it was our turn, I decided to take a different track.

I saw the full venue as an opportunity to fulfill my responsibility to Klaus Kroner. As the boys huddled behind me onstage, I locked the microphone in my left myoelectric hand and paused, then addressed the now silent group.

"In my day as a player, our cleats came in one color: black. And our uniform shorts were... well, short." I drew an imaginary short-shorts line across my upper right thigh. "Back then, as players, we were charged with educating the public, the media, and the young players about this beautiful game."

After another pause to ensure I had secured everyone's silence and attention, I continued.

"I left my professional coaching career to return to my roots. In youth soccer, it seems the pendulum has swung backward—and my style is now considered old school."

I began to pace the stage, making what eye contact I could with the audience seated in the dimmed theater, past the near-blinding stage lights.

"You could benefit from being a little old school yourselves," I told the players in the crowd. "You don't need to wear the most expensive cleats. You don't need coaches to direct your every move. All you need is a ball and a wall."

I stopped in place. "And that doesn't mean the door of your garage."

The audience—I assume mostly the parents—broke out in laughter.

"Call your friends and get games going at a nearby soccer field, at the schoolyard, or at the biggest backyard in your neighborhood. Turn off your brain and play from your heart."

I turned back to face my mongrels. "These boys learned to do just that and proved with their success how talented they are. I'm immensely proud of these players and the people they have become—and will become."

Also onstage was Richard Peters. He lurked near where the boys had lined up, as if standing guard to keep them on point. I held his gaze as I said, "Even as a C-level team, they deserve the respect of everyone in the club."

Looking again to my group of hooligans, I ended with, "Thank you, gentlemen. I learned a lot from you."

A few weeks later, tryouts for the next season were held. Twelve of my seventeen boys advanced to the upper teams; eight went on to the B team and four to the A team. Because so many of my guys were promoted, the C team was disbanded.

As for me, I wasn't asked to return—no email, no text, no phone call. No communication of any sort. No acknowledgment for my time, and nothing more than a few of my fellow coaches shaking my hand and thanking me for speaking up during the season-ending gathering.

Looking back, I'm not sure if those kids needed me more than I needed them, or if it was the other way around. I guess it doesn't matter. But I hope they found that I was good on my word—that I didn't teach them much at all. I only put them each in a position to learn.

Life's a road trip; sometimes we follow a map, and other times we just wing it. And at the end, we often return to familiar roads —roads we know well but travel again later with a renewed sense of perspective.

Six months later, I returned to Wisconsin and won another state championship with a different group of soccer rats. Oh, and guess what? Sue from JC and I are happily married. Her smile still lights up her eyes, and she still looks great in a worn pair of blue jeans.

The Author

Alongside his role as a soccer coach, author Scott Martin has returned to the classroom as a teacher in Wisconsin. He is a well-known advocate for the disability community—a passion he channels through his podcast, *Life's a Road Trip*. Martin holds an Advanced National Coaching License and brings more than thirty years of experience coaching soccer at the select youth, high school, and college levels. He has been named Coach of the Year four times and has led teams to two state championships. Most recently, Martin was appointed a Global Advisor to Billion Strong, a worldwide disability advocacy organization.